D1259876

Theology and Science in
Mutual Modification

Theology and Science in Mutual Modification

by

Harold P. Nebelsick

New York
Oxford University Press
1981

Copyright © 1981 by Christian Journals Limited.

Library of Congress Cataloging in Publication Data

Nebelsick, Harold P, 1925 –
  Theology and science in mutual modification.

  (Theology and scientific culture; 2)
  Bibliography: p.
  Includes index.
  1. Religion and science – History of controversy.
I. Title II. Series.
BL245.N43 261.5'5 81-16932
ISBN 0-19-520273-2 AACR2

Printing (last digit): 987654321
Printed in Great Britain

Contents

To MELISSA
whose care, concern and diligence
has made this book possible.

General Foreword

The appearance of a series of books on *Theology and Scientific Culture* indicates that we are moving beyond the old antithesis between theology and science, and that the disastrous split in our western culture between the natural and the human sciences is in process of being healed. The increasing pervasiveness of science in our modern life is due not merely to the impact of new technologies on our everyday existence, but to the fact that science has been throwing up integrative modes of thought which have far-reaching implications for knowledge in every sphere of human enterprise. To a unifying outlook of this kind theology has much to offer, as in dialogue with natural science it gains a deeper understanding of the creation through which God makes himself known to mankind. Moreover, it is more and more being realised by natural science through dialogue with theology that empirico-theoretical science as we have developed it owes not a little to the injection of Judaeo-Christian ideas about the universe and its contingent order into the framework of its regulative beliefs.

The day is fast receding when people regarded theology and science as mutually exclusive or when the natural sciences were despised by the humanities as having little to do with the finer and more intangible levels of human life and thought. All sciences, human, natural and theological, share the same concern for the integrity, authenticity and beauty of the universe in which God has placed us, the same passion for objectivity and truth in our multivariable relations with reality, and the same call for humility born of the conviction that the created order manifests a range of intelligibility that we may apprehend only at its comparatively elementary levels. Yet the more deeply we probe into the secrets of the universe, the more we become locked into a dimension of intelligibility that transcends its manifestations in the phenomenal patterns of nature and makes them point indefinitely beyond themselves. As our scientific inquiries press hard upon the boundaries of created reality, we find ourselves grasped by a commanding rationality calling for universal respect and commitment beyond the limits of our scientific experience and formalisable knowledge. As the universe unfolds the simplicity, harmony and subtlety of its order to our questioning, the more it is heard to cry out for its Creator. Thus theological and scientific inquiry have begun to overlap and bear upon each other at decisive points. We have entered upon a new age in which we are compelled to reject the old dualisms, change our received notions, and develop richer, unifying forms of thought, more adequate to an enlarged apprehension of the nature of the universe and its transcendent Creator.

The theologians and scientists who contribute to this series are all very different in training and outlook and in religious persuasion. But they all share the same concern to bridge the gap between theology and science and to find ways of developing dialogue between them on a constructive basis. There are no overall directives. Each contributor has been invited to take his own way, so that none is committed to the views of another through sharing in the same enterprise. It is hoped that in this way an open and fruitful dialogue will emerge in which many others beyond the immediate contributors to this series may take part.

In this book Dr Harold P. Nebelsick, who is Professor of Doctrinal Theology at Louisville Presbyterian Theological Seminary, Louisville, Kentucky, comes at the problems that face us today from behind, by disentangling the confused interconnections between theology and natural science which have affected the outlook of the Western world since the rise and dominance of Newtonian thought. He is concerned to clear the ground not only for fresh dialogue but for a more constructive grasp of the mutual dependence of theological and scientific concepts. He is particularly well qualified to do this, in view of his wide training and experience on both sides of the Atlantic and his many years of participation in inter-disciplinary discussion in international and ecumenical circles. This is the first of several volumes on which he has been working for some time.

Thomas F. Torrance

Preface

Theologians from Augustine to Barth have called theology "a science". Barth calls it "the most thankful and happy of sciences". For the most part, however, since the demise of Newtonianism with its deistic conceptualities, theology has chosen to ignore science as being outside its scope of concern.

In the early part of the twentieth century voices as different as those of Ernst Troeltsch, Karl Heim and Alfred North Whitehead were raised to contest the dichotomy between science and theology. They themselves, however, were too much fettered by idealistic conceptualities to influence main stream theology into thought patterns which were conversant with those of modern science. Even Karl Barth, the giant among twentieth-century theologians, finds natural science outside the immediate concern of theology in spite of the urgings of his two friends, Heinrich Scholz and Günter Howe, to the contrary. The situation seems to be changing for the better, however. Wolfhart Pannenberg and Gerhard Sauter have made important contributions in exposing the hiatus between theology and natural science and pointing to the necessity of bridging the gap between the two areas of thought. Stanley Jaki's historical investigations are extremely helpful in showing the relationship of science to theology. Mary Hesse analyses the problem of knowledge in science in ways that may be applicable to theology. Arthur Peacocke attempts to bridge the science-theology gap with an empirical analysis. Ian Barbour continues to point out the more important issues in science as over against religion in general. Following process philosophy, however, his thought continues to be caught in Whiteheadian categories. Michael Polanyi has shown the necessity of the personal aspect of scientific decision-making and the necessity of a fiduciary stance in natural science which parallels the "confessional aspect" of theological thinking. The theologian and philosopher of science Thomas F. Torrance draws on the history of both science and theology as well as the categories of Einsteinian science in an attempt to penetrate into the rationality of reality with which both natural science and theology must occupy themselves. C. F. von Weizsäcker and A. M. Klaus Müller consider Heisenberg and Bohr to have moved beyond Einstein in stressing the necessary inter-dependence of subject and object in the thought structures of natural science in particular and hold that this implies an interdependence of subject and object in all epistemological processes.

With this as background, my thesis is threefold: (1) The present dichotomy between natural science and theology is both debilitating and unnecessary. (2) The history of the development of the two disciplines, especially since the rise of seventeenth-century science which eventuated in a closed and self-sufficient understanding of the world, encouraged a bad marriage between science and theology, on the one hand, and a divorce between the two, on the other. (3) In view of the new conceptions of world reality brought to light by relativity and quantum physics, we are now entering a time when dialogue and fruitful conversations between theology and science are possible and are being pursued.

I have been fortunate to be a member of faculty at Louisville Presbyterian Theological Seminary whose generous sabbatical policy, along with a grant from the Advanced Religious Study Foundation sponsored by Mr and Mrs Lawrence H. Favrot, has enabled me to spend fifteen months in research at the University of Göttingen, 1975-1976, and eight months at the University of Edinburgh, 1980. I am grateful for both these institutions who granted me visiting professor status, opened library and research facilities to me and enabled me to have helpful and encouraging conversations with members of faculty. I owe a special debt of gratitude to Professor T. F. Torrance who is both my "Doctor Father" and the editor of the series in which these lines are published. He has both led me into this research and encouraged me to go in the direction my research has taken me, this in addition to the meticulous work he has done in editing the following text for publication. In view of my frequent references to his writings in the ensuing pages it may be worth noting that these were made in the original draft well before I had any inkling that he was planning a series in which this work could be included. I am also grateful to Mr Eyre Crowe of Edinburgh for copy-editing the typescript in preparation for its final draft.

Most of all I am indebted to my wife, Melissa, who has endured the impatience of a husband whose assessment of time needed for a project is usually a fraction of that which turns out to be necessary. She has kept things in order, typed draft after draft of this manuscript and has spent hour after hour in the libraries of Edinburgh checking the references and quotations in preparation for publication. I am doubly grateful because she enjoys working with the books at least as much as I.

I have tried to keep foreign expressions to a minimum. However, I have retained certain foreign words, phrases and titles and have followed them with English translations when such inclusion helps to specify the work or the meaning of the text and especially when I judged that such words have become a part of the vocabulary of the informed reader. Titles of foreign books and articles, for the most part, are given in English if the writing has been translated. If not, I have retained the title in the original language and included a translation in parenthesis. With regard to texts from foreign language works, if the reference to the work is given in the original language, the translation is my own; if the reference is in English, the text is from the English edition cited.

Harold P. Nebelsick

Edinburgh, July 1981.

Chapter I

The Present Perspective

Beginning at the Beginning

It is a truism to say ours is the "scientific-technological age". A statement so true in itself, however, is not altogether or exclusively true. Although science and technology dominate our time, ours is not the only age that has been affected by science and technology. If science is the way that we conceptually appreciate the order of the world and re-order it and technology is the "handmaiden" by which this ordering and re-ordering is carried out, then science and technology are as old as is the human species itself. From the time humankind became humankind, they have seen order in their universe and re-ordered it. When they, as is supposed, surveyed the savannah from the trees and then, following their vision, moved out of the treetops on to the topography of the plain, they were on the way to developing science and technology. As they differentiated small rocks and sticks from large ones, loose rocks and sticks from fixed ones, picked up the former to strike and dislodge the latter or to attack or ward off an adversary, they both became aware of the "given order" of their environment and began to shape it into a "new order".

Thus the scientific, technological process began. The stick became a club, the rock the hand axe. Fitted together the handled axe was made. The first spears, simply pointed sticks, were "improved upon" when the stick was "pointed" with a knapped stone. The atlatl elongated the throw-arm and extended the range of the spear. Then came the bow, the arrow, the plow, the harness, the boat, the wheel, the wagon, the chariot, the sail, the windmill, the compass, gunpowder, the rocket, the cannon, the sextant, the pendulum, the telescope, the steam engine, etc., etc.

As order was recognized, new order was conceived and new tasks were designated. Concept gave rise to tool and tool to concept. Thus science and technology, though they were largely unconscious to those responsible for their development, combined to facilitate the discernment of "order" and the making of "order". As humankind moved over the land, first as hunter and gatherer and later as farmer and herdsman, they used tools to fulfil their goals and thought of new goals for which their tools were necessary. New thought demanded new tools and vice versa. Knowledge was passed on from father to son, from mother to daughter. The body of knowledge as to *what* and *how* formed itself into tradition by which the world was identified and handled. Science, the conscious conceptual ordering of reality, began to be born. Transferred to the making of tools and their use, it became knowledge of technique— "technology".

Tribes transformed themselves into communities, communities into cities. The land was settled, divided and tilled. Agricultural efficiency provided the means for existence beyond constant toil and allowed first for leisure and learning and eventually for class structures in which leisure and learning were pursued. As tribes expanded into nations, security from want as well as hostility was provided by technology. People's thoughts moved from providing the basic necessities of life to dreams and the study of the beyond. Surpluses of food and products of technology from flints to pots were made for trade. Friendly intercourse ensued between peoples and with it came the exchange of knowledge. The Babylonians studied the stars. The Greeks improved upon Babylonian mathematics and applied it to the movement of the heavens as well as to the measurements of the earth.

Through the centuries knowledge accrued, sometimes halting and moving back on itself, later to recuperate and move forward again. With the age of Pericles (*c.* 490–429 B.C.), Greece had reached its apogee both in science and in

philosophy of which science itself was a part. Greek learning
was preserved by Plato (427?–347 B.C.) and by Aristotle
(384–322 B.C.). Platonic thought was incorporated into the
theology of the early Church and with the Church it moved into
the West. Aristotelian thought, acquired and preserved by the
Arabs who brought it to Spain, was synthesized with the
theology of the Middle Ages and helped to form the medieval
western mind. With Aristotelian philosophy came Aristotelian
science and by it the classical world was conceived in the womb
of the Christian West bringing forth first the Renaissance and
later the Reformation. The Greek impetus to investigate the
world and the Reformation emphasis, which secularized the
world and opened it to investigation, combined to produce the
explosion of science in the seventeenth-century. The world
which could be investigated could also be handled. Investigations called for instrumentation; instrumentation opened the
way to new investigation. Knowledge combined with technique
produced machines for the investigations of science as well as
for industry. Industry (applied technology) called for power
beyond that provided by water and wind. In 1776, a little more
than two centuries ago, James Watt (1736–1819) incorporated
the mechanical innovations of Thomas Savery (1650?–1715)
and Thomas Newcomen (1663–1729), his immediate predecessors, in fabricating the first industrially viable steam engine.
The power of fire, transmuted by steam into practical use (long
after it was first incorporated by Hero of Alexandria (c. 130
B.C.) in his steam-fired rotating globe and the hot air shrine
door opener), thus gave birth to the scientific-technological
age.[1]

The Dichotomy Between Science and Theology

Although in a real sense modern science and technology had
been building up in a significant way since the beginnings of the
thirteenth-century, the impact of the seventeenth-century
breakthrough into the era of modern science was such that we
do well to take the English mathematician-philosopher Alfred
North Whitehead (1861–1947) seriously when he says that
only the Babe in the manger created a greater thing than that
caused by the emergence of natural science in the

seventeenth-century.[2] So great was the impact of this development that today we cannot possibly think of our lives or the
lives of peoples, cultures, nations, or of the planet itself,
without thinking in terms of science any more than we can
think of the Middle Ages without thinking of Christianity, the
Renaissance without the revival of classical thought, or of
Protestantism and its influence upon government and culture
without the Reformation. As the apostle Paul, according to
Luke, the author of Acts, cited the early third century B.C. Stoic
poet Aratus (*Phaenomena* 1.5), "In him we live and move and
have our being" (Acts 17:28), to expound the ubiquity of God
to the Greeks, so we may perhaps say, at least as far as our
earthly existence is concerned, "We live and move and have
our being under the aegis of science and technology".

Yet, in spite of the ubiquity and the pervasive influence of
science and technology, we, whose calling it is to think in terms
of faith and theology, somehow imagine that we can do without
science as far as our thinking is concerned. Though we admire
its thought structures and live under its beneficence, we are
more likely than not to revile it, neglect it, or reject its
implications. In theology, by and large, we have imbibed the
idea that science and technology, if not dangerous to the faith,
are not "faith's concern". The result is that those of us who
have grown up in the western world, especially those of us who
take the Christian faith seriously, have tended to be
schizophrenic. On the one hand, we are aware of the *hard,*
handlable, practical "realities" which we can define, designate,
measure, shape, understand, develop and create through the
means of natural science and technology. On the other hand,
there are the *soft* "realities" of literature, poetry, and religion
such as loyalty, faith, kindness, concern and love. The sharp
cleavage between the realm of natural scientific knowledge and
that with which we are concerned in "the humanities" or in
"religious faith", has given rise to disastrous division among us
resulting, as C. P. Snow (1905–1980) has said, in "the two
cultures".[3] With half our heads we are hard-headed secularists
and with the other half soft-hearted admirers of the arts and
adherents to faith. Many of us are both at one and the same
time or both at different times depending on the demands of
the occasion. The Heidelberg philosopher Georg Picht

(1913–) can compare our situation to a "conversation" between a person who cannot talk and a person who cannot see.

> The dialogue between religion and secular thinking is like a conversation between a person who is dumb and a person who is blind. The one who is dumb cannot say what he sees. The one who is blind can only say what he doesn't see.[4]

The argument I shall try to put forward in the following pages is that the collective schizophrenia between what we in the Anglo-Saxon world refer to as "the arts" or "the humanities" on the one hand and "the sciences" on the other will not do. It is at one and the same time unneccessary and dangerous. It will not do because our collective schizophrenia is in reality collective insanity which, considering the tools now available, could very easily lead to our collective self-destruction. Especially to those of us who are of the Judaeo-Christian tradition, this divided mind is unnecessary and must be seen as unnecessary. Both the Judaeo-Christian doctrines of creation and of salvation comprise a concept of wholeness in which all aspects of reality including human reality impinge on one another and are mutually modifying. The truth of faith, then, must correlate with or be complementary to the truth of science. Though each discipline has its own particular preserve, faith and science cannot be judged as being either incidental or adverse to one another. If incidental to one another, one or both must be judged as irrelevant. If inconsistent with one another, one or both must be judged inadequate and ultimately invalid.

An indication of the deep and dangerous hiatus to which we have referred is given by the Roman Catholic philosopher Étienne Gilson (1884–1978) in his statement, "Nothing equals the ignorance of the modern philsophers in matters of science, except the ignorance of modern scientists in matters of philosophy".[5] Were we to substitute the word "theologians" for the word "philosophers", we would have reflected the sad but actual state of the major voices of theology of our time and not only of our time but of much of the time since the rise of seventeenth-century science.

Philosophy's and especially theology's ignorance and mistrust of natural science are at least somewhat understandable when we realize that the development of modern science, though enhanced for a time by the philosophy of René Descartes (1596–1650), was given a dualistic and, hence, eventually disruptive slant by the presuppositions of Cartesianism. Descartes' attempt to construct a universal science with the same certainty displayed by mathematics led him to reject all traditional teaching, and to doubt all that was not indubitable. Since the *self* that doubts cannot doubt the self, the "I" who thinks *(cogito)* is the first of Descartes' *lucid* concepts by which reality is to be known. God, who also is not subject to doubt and is responsible for the correlation of ideas with reality, is the second. And then there are the objects of reality apprehended with clarity and certainty through acts of intuition. These are arranged in an analytic system beginning with the simple, self-evident truths which are found near at hand and range to the more complicated and remote principles according to set rules which were thought to yield rational and universal knowledge. Since the system called for dividing the *res cogitans* (thinking reality or the self) from the *res extensa* (reality as thought or reality as extended outside the mind), reality was necessarily and effectively split between subject and object.

Further, in that objects, to be objects of reality, must be clearly intuited by mind, this separation of "the subject" or reality *(res cogitans*–the thinking reality *within the observer)* from "the object" of reality *(res extensa*–reality thought about *outside the observer)* split nature down the middle. The subject, the self, was of the realm of mind or spirit. The mind was non-corporeal. That which the mind apprehended, its objects, were the substances of the physical world which were arranged uniformly and mechanically and could thus be known by a process of analysis which demanded simplicity along with rigidity.[6]

Little wonder, then, that as the sciences developed there came about a split between the human sciences or philosophy, theology, and the arts and the natural sciences or the disciplines dealing with "the world out there". Descartes' scheme led to the domination of "subject" over "object" to such an extent that eventually objects became subjectified, completely dominated by the mind or the self.

Descartes' bifurcation of reality into subjectivity and objectivity and his subjectivization of reality to the concepts of mind were further developed or rather systematized by Immanuel Kant (1725–1804). According to his idealistic scheme the mind is differentiated from reality which it conceives, but in conceiving reality, and ordering its conceptions of it through the *a priori* categories of understanding, the mind *is creative* of the very order by which reality is known. Hence mind becomes responsible for the *phenomena* of reality, i.e., of things as they appear to us.

As the idealistic arrangement continues, it is given historical validity and thus substantiation by Wilhelm Dilthey (1833–1911). According to Dilthey, the differentiation between the *Naturwissenschaften* (the natural sciences) and the *Geisteswissenschaften* (the human sciences) has been part and parcel of the culture and thought of the western world from the beginning. The differentiation is not only legitimate but, considering the construction of the world as we know it, it is inevitable. Thus the Cartesian-Kantian-Diltheian differentiation between the natural sciences, on the one hand, and the human sciences, on the other (with theology being considered for the most part as belonging to the latter), evolves into a dualistic conceptual framework which runs through western culture as a whole.[7]

Especially in Protestant thought, the *subjectivity* of faith was, and for the most part still is, contrasted with the *objectivity* of natural science. Martin Luther's (1483–1546) emphasis on the *pro me* ("for me") of faith tends to place the believer over against nature, the Church over against the world. The eighteenth-century pietistic stress on the importance and ultimate validity of the "inner life" as over against the world develops into Friedrich Schleiermacher's (1768–1834) dependence upon "feeling" *(das Gefühl)* as the faculty for grasping theological truth. Inspired by the Kantian moral imperative, this subjective approach developed with Albrecht Ritschl (1822–1889) into the "theology of human values". The thought of Wilhelm Herrmann (1846–1922) was based upon an experience-centered inwardness. Adolf von Harnack (1851–1930) moved into an "historicism" which, in interpreting the past in terms of what it means for us in the present,

subjectivizes history. In our time the theologies of Rudolf
Bultmann (1884–1976) and of Paul Tillich (1886–1965),
informed by an existentialist philosophy centered on self-
consciousness, continue the trend.[8]

Perhaps this critique of subjectivity applies in a more subtle
way to those theologies which emphasize "salvation history" to
the neglect of world history as exemplified by such scholars as
Oscar Cullmann (1900–   ) and George Ernest Wright
(1909–1974). To a certain extent the criticism is also applicable to the most profound of modern theologians, Karl Barth
(1886–1968), whose "Theology of the Word" tends to be
centered on the believer and the community of faith rather
than on history or world-reality. All these, it would seem, even
those who in no sense wanted to split theology off from natural
science as such, grew up on a debilitating diet of the "human
sciences" to the neglect of the "natural sciences".

The protest of Karl Heim (1874–1958) against the isolation
of theology from philosophy (though Heim's own idealism
promised to be no cure) may be taken as a warning against the
isolation of theology from the world of thought:

> It was a disastrous turning point in the history of Protestantism
> when Protestant theology, shortly after Schleiermacher, cut
> itself loose from its link with philosophy. Since then it has more
> and more withdrawn from the difficult task of placing the
> world-view of faith over against that of unfaith. It thereby
> satisfied itself with the task of extracting the central concern (the
> *Heilsgeschichte*–salvation history) from the total picture of real-
> ity, which picture every believing person must have if he is to act
> responsibly within this world . . . Theology, then, proceeded to
> develop this central concern in every direction believing it could
> confidently leave everything else to the profane sciences.[9]

It is this disastrous decision to neglect the thought world of
science and technology which, perhaps more than any other
factor, has brought about the present hiatus between the "two
cultures". Much of what was once called "the Christian world"
now judges the Church as an antiquated institution, good for
holding one's hand in times of doubt and death, perhaps, but
hardly the place to which the majority now turn for answers to
life or strength to meet basic problems. Manfred Eigen
(1927–   ), who was awarded the Nobel Prize in Biology in

1967, and his co-worker, Ruthold Winkler (1941–   ) of the University of Göttingen, have expressed this indictment of theology in cogent terms:

> Theology, insofar as it expresses itself as a science, satisfies itself for the most part with the transmission and explanation of an historical reservoir of thought. Contributions to the doctrines of morals and mores are today more likely to be expected from those branches of science other than theology.[10]

The critique may be too harsh, and although theology should not claim to be primarily interested in morals and social matters, it is often the case that theology seems content to occupy itself in delving into the past to find a supposed once-for-all truth. It makes a science out of the exegesis and interpretation of the texts of Scripture and those of church history, as it well should. It attempts to systematize its belief systems and legitimize these on the basis of tradition. For the most part, however, it continues to neglect natural science and the scientific conceptions of reality which, whether we like it or not, have in our day appropriated the place theology once had in shaping the world in which we live and the minds of those who live in it.[11]

The Dominance of Science

Thus, with or without present theological input, and usually without it, science and technology continue to extend their domain. Professor Stanley Jaki (1924–   ) has pointed out that already at the turn of the century, in 1897 to be exact, the French chemist Marcelin Berthelot (1827–1907) in something of an overstatement reflected a ubiquity of scientific influence:

> People begin to understand that in the modern civilization, every social utility derives from science, because modern science embraces the entire domain of the human mind: the intellectual, moral, political, artistic domain as well as the practical and industrial.[12]

In the same vein, the British historian Herbert Butterfield (1900–   ) corroborates Whitehead's judgement, mentioned above, in emphasizing the importance of natural science as it evolved out of the seventeenth-century scientific revolution.

The seventeenth-century, indeed, did not merely bring a new factor into history, in the way we often assume – one that must just be added, so to speak, to the other permanent factors. The new factor immediately began to elbow at the other ones, pushing them out from their places – and, indeed, began immediately to seek control of the rest, as the apostles of the new movement had declared their intention of doing from the very start. The result was the emergence of a kind of Western civilisation which when transmitted to Japan operates on tradition there as it operates on tradition here – dissolving it and having eyes for nothing save a future of brave new worlds. It was a civilisation that could cut itself away from the Graeco-Roman heritage in general, away from Christianity itself – only too confident in its power to exist independent of anything of the kind. We know now that what was emerging towards the end of the seventeenth-century was a civilisation exhilaratingly new perhaps, but strange as Nineveh and Babylon. That is why, since the rise of Christianity, there is no landmark in history that is worthy to be compared with this.[13]

Likewise, the mathematician and philosopher Professor Günter Howe (1908–1968) points out that, "whereas we tend to write history from the point of view of political struggle or military catastrophe, to no powers on earth was it given so to change the earth as did Kepler and Galileo with the physical technical development that began with them, the ramifications of which reach out to the remotest areas of China and India".[14] Looking at the scientific, technical revolution in the light of its consequences, Arnold Gehlen (1904–   ) can compare it to the so-called "neolithic revolution" when humankind moved from the hunter and gatherer to the farmer and herdsman and thus opened the way to further cultural development.[15]

Little wonder, then, that science and technology are often considered to be a "religious phenomenon". The physicist and philosopher C. F. von Weizsäcker (1912–   ) calls it "a universal religion".[16] We believe in it, trust it, live according to its dictates and expect it to prolong our lives and to save us from calamity. Thus 150 years after the French philosopher Auguste Comte (1798–1857) published his essay, *Considérations sur la pouvoir spirituelle* ("Considerations Regarding the Spiritual Power") in 1826, his prophecy that science was the "'new spiritual power' that was destined to exercise an even greater influence over temporal affairs than did the Church at the height of her influence in the Middle Ages", seems to have been fulfilled.[17]

Sacred Science

Modern Science did not begin as a substitute or even as a competitor to the Christian faith. As is quite obvious from the history of the development of science, the leading figures of the seventeenth-century scientific movement not only knew themselves to be true sons of the Church, but were certain that their observations of and conclusions about nature were *a service of God*.[18] Though it was not long before science struck out on its own to become a substitute religion, a "universal religion", to repeat Weizsäcker, in the beginning it was not so. For Francis Bacon (1561–1626) the pursuit of science was compared to the practice of faith.[19] Galileo Galilei (1564–1642) attempted to weave theology and astronomy into a single cloth by supporting his astronomical discoveries with biblical citations. Johannes Kepler (1571–1630), like no other it would seem, was certain that his investigation into the harmony of the spheres was God-inspired. Though Kepler had abandoned theological studies for science, he was convinced that the knowledge of God which he read off the order of the heavens was not inferior to that which could be read out of the Scriptures. The prayer with which he ended his *Harmonies of the World, Book 5* indicates both his genuine piety and his confidence in the correlation of his mathematical computation of the movements of the planets with God's own creative activity.

> I give thanks to Thee, O Lord Creator, Who hast delighted me with Thy makings and in the Works of Thy hands have I exulted. Behold! now, I have completed the work of my profession, having employed as much power of the mind as Thou didst give me; to the men who are going to read those demonstrations I have made manifest the glory of Thy works, as much of its infinity as the narrows of my intellect could apprehend. My mind has been given over to philosophizing most correctly: if there is anything unworthy of Thy designs brought forth by me — a worm born and nourished in a wallowing place of sins — breathe into me also that which Thou dost wish men to know, that I may

make the correction: If I have been allured into rashness by the wonderful beauty of Thy works, or if I have loved my own glory among men, while I am advancing in the work destined for Thy glory, be gentle and merciful and pardon me; and finally deign graciously to effect that these demonstrations give way to Thy glory and the salvation of souls and nowhere be an obstacle to that.[20]

Given the "God-dominated" frame of mind the seventeenth-century, which led people to deem God responsible in one way or another for all events and especially those of cosmic dimension, it is not at all surprising that a synthesis between theology and science was considered necessary and was taken for granted from the outset. To reiterate instances: Kepler was certain that the harmony of the heavens reflected the inner being of God himself. Galileo in all sincerity dedicated his *Saggiatore,* in which he erroneously explained the comets as atmospheric emanations reflecting sunlight rather like a halo or a rainbow, to Pope Urban VIII (*c.* 1568–1644). Robert Boyle's (1627–1691) contribution was a volume entitled *The Wisdom of God Manifested in the Works of Creation.* By the time a second edition of the *Principia* became necessary, Isaac Newton (1642–1727) added the "General Scholium" in which he indicated that his "proofs of God", made on the basis of his physics, were as important to him as the laws of physics themselves.

For Newton God was not only necessary to shift the planets of Jupiter and Saturn around from time to time to prevent a cosmic collision; God was built into the rational scheme by which the universe is explained.[21] Newton's pages and pages of "theology", many more than he wrote about natural science, eventually interconnect God and nature. The universe, though created by God and contingent upon him, is, nevertheless, synthesized with God's "sensorium", the space and time in which God is present to things. God and the world thus became so interconnected that the nature of God can be read out of the order of nature.

Newtonianism

Newtonianism, an amalgamation of natural science and theology, began with John Ray (1627–1705), the father of

English natural history. Beginning in 1690 with the first of his *Three Physico-Theological Discourses,* Ray called upon the new science in general and Newtonian physics in particular to prove the existence and nature of God from the order of nature. Ray was followed by John Toland (1670–1722) whose deistic concept of God paralleled that of Newton and who incorporated Newtonian principles in his *Christianity Not Mysterious* (1696). God, Toland claimed and proclaimed, was the designer of the universe, the original mechanic who constructed it all. He was, therefore, worthy of worship. Ray restricted God's continuing activity, however, to intervening from time to time for necessary repairs. William Derham (1657–1735) continued to display arguments from design in both his *Physico-Theology* in 1713 and *Astro-Theology* in 1714. God, the designer, was read off the universe, the order and regularities of which were considered to be characteristic of the Creator himself. Matthew Tindal (1656–1733) continued the theme with his *Christianity as Old as Creation* (1730) indicating that the foundations of the faith were to be found in the order which the world had now and was thought to have had from the beginning.

The message was delivered even more emphatically from the pulpit by Richard Bentley (1622–1742) in a series of sermons in 1692 under the Robert Boyle Lectureship.[22] Bentley, especially in Sermons VII and VIII which, along with VI, were entitled, "A Confutation with Atheism from the Origin and Frame of the World", emphasized in the strongest terms the advantages afforded to "natural theology" by Newton's physics. Isaac Newton, "that excellent and divine theorist", had not only demonstrated the relationship between mass and gravity,[23] but had shown that God, "the immaterial living mind doth inform and actuate the dead matter and support the frame of the world".[24] Since "transverse and violent motion can be only ascribed to the right hand of the most high God, creator of the heaven and earth",[25] God "who always acts geometrically"[26] is responsible for the regular movements of the heavenly bodies, the rotation of the earth in its *orbis magnus* about the sun,[27] its rotation on its own axis, and the location and rotation of the other planets. Even more dramatically, Bentley, like Newton, was convinced that God's direct intervention was necessary from time to time to keep the planets in order. "All is established by that eternal and omnipotent God *that by wisdom hath founded the earth, and by understanding hath established the heavens.*" (Prov. 3:19).[28]

As the Psalmist had proclaimed that "the heavens declare the glory of God" (Ps. 19), so now it was widely believed, Newton proclaimed God's glory and omnipotence by his physics. Newton was thus considered to be the new prophet and when the *Principia* became popular, "Newtonianism", which was first called upon to support religion, was well on its way to becoming "a religion" in its own right.[29] So strong were the effects of this trend of thought that, as we shall see below, they continue into the twentieth-century.[30]

"Newtonian natural theology", though born in Britain was, like Newtonian physics, in no sense confined to the British Isles. As early as 1715, Bernard Nieuwentijdt, a Dutch physician and early-eighteenth-century disciple of Descartes, wrote *Regt gebruik der werelt Beschouwingen,* literally *Correct Application of World-Views.* The book was translated into English by John Chamberlayne and printed under the somewhat bland and rather inexact title, *The Religious Philosopher,* in 1717. Nieuwentijdt, who designed his work "for the conviction of atheists and infidels", is referred to by Chamberlayne as "the learned physician", "the Dutch Ray or Derham" who "like the two English philosophers so well proved the Wisdom, Power and Goodness of God by the strongst Arguments, Observations on Facts and Demonstrations drawn from Experiments".[31]

Like Ray, Nieuwentijdt amassed arguments from botany and zoology. Like Bentley, he called upon the physics of Sir Isaac Newton whose experiments with light and laws of motion he confessed impressed him almost as much as "the most amazing structure of the heavens and all its furniture".[32] Like Bishop Oresme (*c.* 1320–1382) of Paris, he was convinced that "as a clock or any other ingenious piece of workmanship does prove the Skill of the Maker" so the intricacies of the world "prove God as its Maker".[33]

In France, too, Newtonianism was pressed into theological service. Even François Voltaire (1694–1778) who was not known for his piety, went so far as to insist that Newton's theories necessarily led to the knowledge of a " 'superior being who has created everything, arranged everything freely' ".[34] In Germany, Newtonianism moved by way of Kant into philosphical thought where it had and still has tremendous influence. Kant first used Newton's *Principia* as a basis for his *Universal Natural History and Theory of the Heavens* in which he argued for God's existence on the basis of the lawfulness and the order of nature. Later, and more importantly, as will be discussed in some detail below, Kant then "apriorized" Newton's concepts of space and time into categories of the understanding as foundations for his metaphysics.

As late as 1803, three-quarters of a century after Newton's death, Claude-Henri de Saint-Simon (1760–1825), a declassed French noble, wrote a tract *Lettres d'un inhabitant de Genève à ses contemporains* ("Letters from a Citizen of Geneva to his Contemporaries") in which with an enthusiasm which paralleled that of Bentley, he continued to proclaim Newton's truth as God's revelation. The tract called for the founding of a church under scientist-priests and for the erection of temples to Newton which would carry out the orders of the Great Council of Newton and be centers of rational worship, research and instruction.[35] Thus, the argument for God on the basis of the design of the universe, an updated version of Thomas Aquinas' (1225–1274) "five ways" backed by "scientific data", was on its way to becoming the foundation of a popular Protestant rational theology.

Science as "scientism" was a new faith in the making. It was a new orthodoxy based as securely on seventeenth-century science as the orthodoxy of Protestantism was based upon the authority of Scripture or that of the Roman Catholic faith on the authority of the Church. It was an orthodoxy so palpably persuasive and powerful that the French theologian Ernest Renan (1823–1892) could say, "Science and science alone is capable of restoring to humanity that without which it cannot live: a creed and a law".[36] "Science" was the new word. The hope, enthusiasm and optimism of the nineteenth-century were the results. Science would provide "the solution of the enigma, the final explanation to mankind of the meaning of things, the explanation of man to himself".[37] Henceforth, humankind could live securely in the present and look forward to eschatological fulfilment in the future, not a future of uncertainty and doubt, but a future in which *belief would be replaced by knowledge*. Omniscience would replace partial understanding and encompass the totality of life. Scientific procedures would allow the laws of government and human affairs to be ascertained with the same kind of exactitude as the laws of physics.[38] Fulfilment was not yet, of course, but the end was certain because the pattern of the future could be read off the universe in the present.

Marxism

By far the most pertinent and powerful manifestation of the new science as applied to politics was, of course, the dialectical materialism of Karl Marx (1818–1883) and Friedrich Engels (1820–1895). By presupposing an eschatological optimism and basing their "scientific materialism" on the progressive, perfectable, and essentially closed system of seventeenth-century science, Marx and Engels were able to propose an "exact" political science in which the future was presented with the same certainty as the past and present out of which it had developed. As logical extrapolations from the "scientific analogies" of history became inerrant dogmas, political theory became "political religion", the promises of which were as unequivocal as they were universal and the demands of which were to be answered by unswerving obedience.

Marx explained the history of humankind by following an Hegelian scheme according to which history develops dialectically from its beginning to the present with extrapolations into the future. History was regarded as a series of struggles between the upper exploiting and lower exploited classes. The past internecine economic warfare led to the present bourgeoisie-dominated society, with the same kind of determinism displayed by the moon as it passes from phase to phase or by the earth as it moves from season to season in its orbit around the sun, and so the war goes on. However, since the inviolable laws of history predict the inevitable triumph of the working class, the struggles of the past, like those of the present, are bound to lead to the predetermined future victory of the exploited classes through whose effort society has been built. As society passed from the slavery of feudalism and capitalism, so now the advanced political systems have entered the necessary transitional stage of socialism. Sooner or later, and the sooner the better, all societies and political systems will gravitate into the state of pure communism and the freedom of the stateless society where all will be enlightened and each will contribute according to his ability and demand only according to his need.

Marx was as confident of the promise of the future, of an "eschatology" of a better world, in contrast to the wretchedness of the masses in the present, as the early Christians were convinced that the *parousia* (the second coming of Christ) would inaugurate the new age. Since the promised future is as certain as that spring will follow winter, dedication in the present and accompanying privation are a small price to pay for the rewards which are sure to come. Even now recompense can be anticipated by those who are engaged in the process of bringing the promise to its fulfilment. "What the bourgeoisie, therefore, produces above all are its own grave diggers. Its fall and the victory of the proletariat are equally inevitable."[39] Hence the trumpet call: "The proletarians have nothing to lose but their chains. They have a world to win. Working men of all countries, unite."[40]

God, of course, is not only superfluous but, in promising to do for humankind what humankind must do for themselves, i.e., change their circumstances and the world, God is a hindrance to the hard-headed recognition of reality. In encouraging patient suffering under the repressive *status quo* in the hope of reward in a future life, religion prevents dealing with the evils of this life. Religion, therefore, is reactionary; it is "the opiate of the people". For the common good, therefore, communism "abolishes all religion".[41]

We may think of Marxism as naïve, and it does, in fact, offer simple answers to extremely complicated questions (a simplicity which, like that of a revivalist's "evangelicalism", makes it easy to comprehend and gives it its popular strength). It would not be popular, however, if its analysis of economic exploitation, like Newtonian science, did not appear to the popular mind in some way to square with "the facts". The economic systems of the world are far from being fair. The poor exist and the exploited too. Ultimately, however, like Newtonian science itself and the philosophies of Kant and Hegel, Marxism will not do.[42] Though it is persuasive and has the status of a substitute religion, Marxism, like the scientism on which it is based, cannot help but provide its adherents with distorted conceptualities and false answers, answers which, as Karl Popper has pointed out, eventuate in either *domination* or *submission*.[43]

For the purpose of our argument at this juncture, Marxism represents the logical end of the process which, stemming from seventeenth-century science, tried to prove God from irrelevant evidence. God was first thought to have been served by science. He was then tied to it and proved by its laws. In the course of development he was relegated to the role of Creator and First Principle, the uncaused Cause who intervened in the universe only in emergency cases ("the God of the gaps"). Finally, when the world was seen to function perfectly well without such emergency interventions, God was judged to be unnecessary and even detrimental to the scientific understanding of reality.

Noting that Newton allowed God "the first impulse but forbade him any further interference in his solar system", Engels wrote with obvious glee:

> God is nowhere treated worse than by natural scientists who believe in him . . . God is treated by his defenders as Frederick William III was treated by his generals and officials in the campaign of Jena. One division of the army after another lowers its weapons, one fortress after another capitulates before the march of science, until at last the whole infinite realm of nature is conquered by science, and there is no place left in it for the Creator.[44]

Engels' judgement of the process leading to God's "redundancy" was quite correct in spite of his misreading of Newton who needed God not only as "first impulse" but, because he could not explain the perturbations of the planets, Newton needed God constantly to regulate the solar system. Indeed, as stated above, Newton believed that the perturbations of Jupiter and Saturn were "of such gravity that divine intervention alone kept the planets in their orbits".[45]

For our purposes it is well to point out that the basis of

Engels' claim regarding God's redundancy came from science itself well before Engels made his début as Marx's compatriot. Working on the mathematics of Joseph Lagrange (1736–1813), the French astronomer Pierre Laplace (1749–1827), "the Newton of France", was able to explain the irregularities in the paths of Jupiter and Saturn as repeatable and predictable periodicities. The perturbations involved were shown to be the result of the inter-relationships in the gravitational attraction between the sun and the planets themselves. Lagrange's mathematical analysis showed the irregularities to be self-correcting in a periodicity of 929+ years. Laplace was thus able to "prove" that Newton's intervening God was quite unnecessary to the understanding of planetary motion. With that argument, as far as science was concerned, God became redundant. Laplace's words regarding God (allegedly in reply to Napoleon's query as to the need for God in an explanation of the universe), *Sire, je n'ai pas eu besoin de cette hypothèse* ("Sire, I have not had need of that hypothesis"),[46] reflect the end of an era.

Aristotle's God, the cryptic God of a good many Christians of the time, the God who capriciously intervened in the processes of nature, was dead. In the mood of Friedrich Nietzsche (1844–1900), science had killed him and, if not the "superman", certainly "superscience" was born. Laplace's words, as Jaki has pointed out, though sounding perhaps "blasphemous to some pious ears . . . reflect a thoroughly sound scientific attitude".[47] They are, as a matter of fact, of such theological import that Dietrich Bonhoeffer (1906–1945) could repeat them from his prison cell in Berlin-Tegel as reflecting a necessary attitude of faith. Bonhoeffer, who at the time was reading C. F. von Weizsäcker's *Zum Weltbild der Physik (The World-View of Physics)* in which Laplace's statement is found, went on to elucidate: *Der Mensch hat gelernt, in allen wichtigen Fragen mit sich selbst, fertig zu werden ohne Zuhilfenahme der Arbeitshypothese Gott.* ("Man has learned in all important questions, to depend upon himself without the aid of the working hypothesis of God.")[48]

John Dewey

As adopted by *scientism,* however, the understanding that the "God hypothesis" was not necessary gave rise to the delusions of a "closed universe". The all-sufficiency of science degenerated into a "dogmatic anti-dogmatism". The American philosopher John Dewey (1859–1952) succinctly illustrated the point. For Dewey the scientific method presents us with nothing less "than a revolution in the 'seat of intellectual authority'".[49] It must be acknowledged, Dewey said, that "there is but one sure road of access to truth—the road of patient cooperative inquiry operating by means of observation, experiment, record and controlled reflection".[50] As such the "scientific method is adverse not only to dogma but to doctrine as well".[51] *"Doctrine"* in its usual meaning is defined by Dewey as "a body of definite beliefs that need only to be taught and learned as true".[52] While *"the method of intelligence"* is open and public . . . the doctrinal method is limited and private".[53] For Dewey "mystical experience", i.e., religious experiences, may have their validity, but as such they are outside the realm of scientific inquiry. Their existence is "an illustration of the general tendency to mark off two distinct realms in one of which science has jurisdiction, while in the other, special modes of immediate knowledge of religious objects have authority".[54] This "dualism", according to Dewey, reiterated the "old dualism between the natural and the supernatural" and *since it is the question of the supernatural which science calls into question,* the circular nature of this type of reasoning and therefore its non-validity were obvious as far as Dewey was concerned.[55]

To reiterate, "classical science", i.e., the science which held from the seventeenth to the end of the nineteenth-century, had largely itself to blame for this state of affairs. While beginning with the legitimate conception that it was being done in the service of God, science soon became responsible for the belief that God could be read off the phenomena of the universe by scientific observation. It then used its "God concept" as an explanation for the unexplainable—*a God of the gaps.* When the gaps were filled, God was pushed out of the universe altogether. "Faith", thus understood, had failed and the doctrines of the faith were replaced by the dogmas proclaiming the closed system of perfectible classical science. There were realities not wholly understood to be sure. But given time and faithfulness to the system, perfect knowledge based upon observation and the understanding of natural law was only a matter of time. With that, "dogmatic science" replaced "dogmatic religion". The results were debilitating not only to the faith but eventually to science as well. Hence, as Weizsäcker has pointed out, "infinity, formerly known of God, is transferred to the world".[56] Just as for Newton space and time constituted God's "sensorium", so "nature now takes the place of God, history is no longer a drama enacted between God and the world, but a process that carries its power and justification within itself".[57] The end of the matter, to refer to Weizsäcker again, is a dialectic of non-reality. "Man no longer hopes for transcendent grace, therefore, he must face nature with optimism, or else despair."[58]

In addition, and as a matter of course, the encapsulization of all reality within the preserve of the observational and measurable stifled any real concern on the part of those engaged in science for any reality that might possibly transcend scientific cognition. This failure to need, or to have contact with, any reality which might transcend nature, as science defined it, went hand in hand with a complacency about the method itself. Nature and the laws of nature which describe reality had for all intents and purposes been discovered. The rest was pure deduction or extrapolation substantiated by experimentation.

Although, as we shall see, one must be careful when quoting Whitehead with regard to modern science,[59] his statements about "scientific dogmatism" serve as a warning that the "scientific method" is as prone to prejudice as any other type of thought. Whitehead thus accuses science of "obscurantism", "the refusal to speculate freely on the limitations of traditional methods".[60]

> Nothing is more curious than the "self-satisfied dogmatism" with which mankind at each period of its history cherishes the delusion of the finality of its existing modes of knowledge, sceptics and believer alike. At this moment scientists and sceptics are the leading dogmatists.[61]

Two Cultures

It would seem, then, that in spite of our sophistication, we still live in the kind of world where our loyalties may very well prevent our minds from assessing reality for what it is. Fixed ideas easily take the place of free thought. With regard to the relationship between natural science and theology, science goes its way and the humanities and theology, by and large, are content to let it go. The result is ignorance and indifference on all sides. Who is to blame for this state of affairs makes little difference. W. Weaver (1894–   ), former president of the American Association of the Advancement of Science, places the larger share of the blame upon scientists themselves, many of whom, he says, are eager enough "to leave their laboratories to talk about things they do *not* understand", while being "pretty reluctant to leave the laboratories to talk and write intelligently about what they *do* superbly understand".[62] On the other hand, C. P. Snow, to whom we referred earlier as having coined the phrase "the two cultures", is certain that scientists are far more aware of the humanities than men of letters are of matters of science, and I tend to agree. Snow accuses the latter of such scientific illiteracy that "the great edifice of modern physics goes up, and the majority of the cleverest people in the western world have about as much insight into it as their neolithic ancestors would have had".[63] With special reference to theology, Georg Picht insists that theology has "hardly taken notice of the forms of science which are responsible for the laws of our time".[64] Understanding itself largely as *Geisteswissenschaft* (human science) in a late-nineteenth-century mode, "theology has reflected very little about the fact that the development of modern science and technology correlates with Christian faith and theological doctrine".[65]

Looking at the German scene in particular, Günter Howe points an accusing finger at the school curriculum itself. Following the Humboldtian educational reforms, which were introduced into German teaching in the early part of the nineteenth-century, the German school system has stressed the instructional worth of classical studies to the neglect of science. The decision was made to opt for the pedagogical power of language, including the grammatical and rhetorical tradition of Gorgias (*c.* 485–*c.* 380 B.C.), Isokrates (436–338 B.C.), Cicero (*c.* 102–43 B.C.) and against Plato's stress on the need to study mathematics. Students from the Humanistic Gymnasia, where those who eventually intend to study theology receive their pre-university education, are thus "robbed of the possibility of being able to understand the scientific, technical world".[66] The result is what Weizsäcker has termed "the deepest split running through the structure of the sciences themselves, the split between the natural sciences and the human sciences".[67] Thus, reality is made to present itself with a bifurcated structure and the Cartesian dichotomy dividing the "subjective" from the "objective" continues.[68]

As Weizsäcker never tires of insisting, however, since "man and nature are integrally related to one another, natural science and human science form two half-circles which must be joined together forming a full circle".[69] The sciences of humanity and those of nature thus complement one another. Therefore, if we are to know reality as a whole, we must consider both halves of the circle as impinging upon and modifying one another.

> On the one side man himself is a natural organism. Nature, however, is older than man . . . but man is older than natural science. Nature was necessary so that man could come into being; man was necessary so that the concepts of nature could come into being.[70]

To know nature, then, is to know nature as integral to ourselves and to know ourselves as integral to nature. If so, it would seem that we have little choice but to see and hold nature and ourselves and ourselves and nature in the closest proximity both conceptually and practically. Only in this way will we who are the conscious part of nature and who, as conscious, are responsible for both the concepts of nature and the reality of nature itself as it is affected by those concepts, be able to know, act and live in inner responsibility with the world. Considering the power that science and technology have put into our hands it would seem quite clear that it is only when we live in inner responsibility with the world that we may be assured that we and the world as we know it will both survive and be enriched. It is intended, after all, that we are "to have life and have it more abundantly" (John 10:10).

Footnotes to Chapter I

1. Watt's engine was preceded by Savery's steam-powered water-raising engine of 1698 and Thomas Newcomen's atmospheric engine of 1705. Neither, however, was considered sufficiently practicable to become viable for industry. The scheme from primitive beginnings to the industrial age follows that of Günter Howe. Cf. below, pp. 166 ff.

2. Alfred North Whitehead, *Science and the Modern World* (Cambridge, 1926), p. 3.

3. C. P. Snow, *The Two Cultures and the Scientific Revolution* (Cambridge, 1959). Though Snow has been criticized for drawing too sharp a dividing line between the "cultures", and especially by Michael Polanyi for not emphasizing the fact that the scientific mind now pervades all culture, making it one, whether we recognize it or not, Snow still has a point. Cf. Michael Polanyi, "The Two Cultures", *Encounter* 13 (March, 1959), 61 ff.

4. Georg Picht, "Umweltschutz und Politik", *Zeitschrift für Rechtspolitik,* 4. Jg. Heft 7 (1971), 137 cited by A. M. Klaus Müller, *Die präparierte Zeit* (Stuttgart, 1970), p. 596.

5. Étienne Gilson, "Science, Philosophy and Religious Wisdom" (The Annual Association Address of the American Catholic Philosophical Association, 1952), *A Gilson Reader,* ed., A. C. Pegis (New York, 1957), p. 217.

6. Cf. René Descartes, *Discourse on Method* in *The Philosophical Works of Descartes,* ed., E. S. Haldane and G. R. T. Ross, 2 vols. (Cambridge, 1967), I, 81-143.

7. Wilhelm Dilthey, *Einleitung in die Geisteswissenschaften,* Sixth Edition, *Gesammelte Schriften,* I (Stuttgart, 1966), 4 ff. Cf. esp. pp. 14-21 for a short explanation of the contradictions between the *Geisteswissenschaften* and the *Naturwissenschaften.*

8. Cf. Albrecht Ritschl, *Three Essays,* translated and introduced by Philip Hefner (Philadelphia, 1972), p. 42 where Hefner shows that Heidegger's programme, which informs the thought of both Tillich and Bultmann, is based upon that of Ritschl.

9. Karl Heim, *Der christliche Gottesglaube und die Naturwissenschaft* (Tübingen, 1949), Eng. tr. (London, 1953), p. 26.

10. Manfred Eigen and Ruthold Winkler, *Das Spiel* (München, 1975), p. 290.

11. Voices, however, are beginning to join that of Professor Whitehead comparing the birth of modern science with that of the Babe born in the manger and that of Heim condemning the disastrous hiatus between theological thinking, on the one hand, and thinking in natural science, on the other. As stated in the preface, Professors T. F. Torrance of Edinburgh, Stanley L. Jaki of Seaton Hall, E. L. Mascall of London, Gerhard Sauter of Bonn, Wolfhart Pannenberg of Munich and Arthur Peacocke of Cambridge, all theologians have written important books on the subject.

12. M. Berthelot, *Science et éducation* (Paris, 1901), p. 13 cited by S. L. Jaki, *The Relevance of Physics* (Chicago, 1970), p. 399.

13. Herbert Butterfield, *The Origins of Modern Science 1300-1800* (London, 1949), p. 174.

14. Günter Howe, *Mensch und Physik* (Berlin, 1963), p. 39.
15. Arnold Gehlen cited by Howe, *Mensch und Physik*, p. 83.
16. Carl Friedrich von Weizsäcker, *Zum Weltbild der Physik* (Stuttgart, 1970), p. 260.
17. Jaki, *Physics*, p. 469.
18. Cf. H. Butterfield, *Origins of Modern Science;* A. C. Crombie, *Augustine to Galileo,* 2 vols. (London, 1957); Thomas F. Torrance, *Theological Science* (London, 1969); R. Hooykaas, *Religion and the Rise of Modern Science* (Edinburgh, 1972), American ed., (Grand Rapids, 1978); *et al.*
19. Francis Bacon, *Novum Organum,* trans. R. Ellis and J. Speeding (London, n.d.), II, lii.
20. Johannes Kepler, *The Harmonies of the World, Book 5, Great Books of the Western World,* Vol. 16 (Chicago, 1952), p. 1080.
21. Isaac Newton, *Opticks* (based on the Fouth Edition, London, 1730: New York, 1952), 3.1, Qu. 31.
22. Richard Bentley, *Eight Sermons* (Oxford, 1809).
23. *Ibid.,* pp. 214 f.
24. *Ibid.,* p. 236.
25. *Ibid.,* p. 242.
26. *Ibid.,* p. 259. This, as well as nearly all of Bentley's "physics", is contained in Newton's four letters to him. Isaac Newton, *The Correspondence of Isaac Newton,* ed., H. W. Turnbull, 7 vols. (Cambridge, 1961), III, 233-256.
27. Bentley, *Eight Sermons,* p. 263.
28. *Ibid.,* p. 290.
29. Cf. Jaki, *Physics,* p. 430 where Jaki speaks of the sealing of a "Holy Alliance" between science and religion.
30. *Ibid.,* pp. 430 ff.
31. Bernard Nieuwentijdt, *The Religious Philosopher,* trans., John Chamberlayne (London, 1717), p. III. The title of the German translation, *Rechter Gebrauch der Weltbetrachtung zur Erkenntnis der Macht, Weisheit und Güte Gottes (The Right Use of the World Conception for the Knowledge of the Power, Wisdom and Goodness of God),* both translates the title correctly and indicates the argument of the author. The French title, *L'Existence de Dieu démontrée par les merveilles de la nature (The Existence of God Demonstrated by the Wonders of Nature),* is equally accurate, if somewhat more succinct. Later English editions add the subtitle, *or the right use of contemplating the works of the Creator.*
32. *Ibid.,* pp. IV, 488, 490.
33. *Ibid.,* p. IV, fn. 56.
34. François Voltaire, *Éléments de la philosophie de Newton,* in *Oeuvres,* XXII, 404, cited by Jaki, *Physics,* p. 432.
35. Claude-Henri de Saint-Simon, "Letters from an Inhabitant of Geneva to his Contemporaries", *Henri Comte de Saint-Simon Selected Writings,* ed. and trans., F. M. H. Markham (Oxford, 1952), pp. 1-11. Cf. Jaki, *Physics,* p. 468.
36. Ernest Renan, *The Future of Science* (London, 1891), p. 24.
37. *Ibid.,* p. 17.

38. *Ibid.*, p. 81.

39. Karl Marx and Friedrich Engels, *Manifesto of the Communist Party, Great Books of the Western World*, Vol. 50 (Chicago, 1952), p. 425.

40. *Ibid.*, p. 434. Thus, in his "Preface to the *Manifesto of the Communist Party* written in 1888, forty years after the original writing, Engels declares, "This proposition, which in my opinion is destined to do for history what Darwin's theory has done for biology, we, both of us, Marx and Engels, had been gradually approaching for some years before 1845", *ibid.*, p. 416.

41. *Ibid.*, p. 428. In modern thought it would seem that Hegel is the first to refer to religion, specifically the Indian, Greek and Roman religions, as having a "narcotic influence". The simile is then adopted by both Bruno and Edgar Bauer, Moses Hess and Ludwig Feuerbach to refer to "religion as opium". Helmut Gollwitzer, *The Christian Faith and the Marxist Criticism of Religion* (Edinburgh, 1970), pp. 15-19.

42. Cf. below, pp. 63 ff. and 71 ff.

43. K. R. Popper, *The Open Society and Its Enemies*, vol. II *The High Tide of Prophecy: Hegel, Marx, and The Aftermath* (London, 1973) p. 276. The book traces Marxism from its Aristotelian and Platonic roots through Hegel and Marx and critiques its implications.

44. Friedrich Engels, *Dialectics of Nature*, trans., Clemens Dutt (London, 1940) pp. 176 f.

45. Cf. Newton, *Opticks*, Qu. 31, pp. 397 ff. where Newton speaks of God as both creating and preserving planetary motion. Cf. also Newton, *Correspondence*, III, 233, 244.

46. Jaki, *Physics*, p. 433.

47. *Ibid.*

48. Dietrich Bonhoeffer, *Widerstand und Ergebung: Briefe und Aufzeichnungen aus der Haft* (München, 1970), p. 215. Cf. English ed., *Letters and Papers from Prison* (London, 1971), p. 325.

49. John Dewey, *A Common Faith* (New Haven, 1960), p. 31.

50. *Ibid.* p. 32.

51. *Ibid.* p. 39.

52. *Ibid.*

53. *Ibid.*, italics added.

54. *Ibid.*, p. 38.

55. *Ibid.*

56. Carl Friedrich von Weizsäcker, *Die Geschichte der Natur* (Göttingen, 1956), p. 48.

57. *Ibid.*, p. 50.

58. *Ibid.*

59. Cf. below, pp. 54 ff.

60. Alfred North Whitehead, *The Function of Reason* (Princeton, 1929), p. 43. This is not to agree with Whitehead's method of "free speculation" on the limitation of method which will be explained in Chapter II and has little place in scientific method.

61. Alfred North Whitehead, "John Dewey and his Influence", *The Philosophy of John Dewey*, ed., Paul Arthur Schilpp (New York, 1939), p. 478. This is not to agree with Whitehead's inadequate understanding of

Einstein's theories of relativity which, as indicated below, really called into question much of Whitehead's process thinking. Cf. below, pp. 54 ff.

62. W. Weaver, "The Imperfections of Science", *Proceedings of the American Philosophical Society* 104 (1960), 427.

63. Snow, *Two Cultures,* p. 15.

64. Georg Picht, *Theologie und Kirche im 20. Jahrhundert* (Stuttgart, 1972), p. 14.

65. *Ibid.,* p. 14 f.

66. Günter Howe, *Gott und die Technik* (Hamburg, 1971) p. 45.

67. Weizsäcker, *Die Geschichte der Natur,* p. 8.

68. *Ibid.* It may be well to point out that this is a different "bifurcation of nature" from that of Whitehead by which he means the distinction between nature as sensed, on the one hand, and that as designated by scientific theory, on the other. Cf. Alfred North Whitehead, *The Concept of Nature* (Cambridge, 1920), pp. 30, 40 and *The Principle of Relativity* (Cambridge, 1922), p. 39.

69. Weizsäcker, *Die Geschichte der Natur,* p. 8. Weizsäcker, however, is careful not to subordinate mind to "nature" as seems to be the case with Whitehead.

70. *Ibid.*

Chapter II

From Natural Theology to Hegelian Idealism

In view of the state of affairs which we discussed in the last chapter, it is understandable that many theologians today suspect any attempt to bridge the gap between theology and natural science. On the one hand, the "substitute religion" thrown up by Newtonian scientism compromised the faith through a natural theology based on order and design. On the other hand, the rejection of scientistic religion and natural theology led to a rejection of science as having any relevance for faith at all. The result was a choice between equally unsatisfactory alternatives.

Argument from Design

In Britain there evolved what Jaki has entitled the "Holy Alliance between science and religion".[1] The attempted unification of science and religion, as indicated above, was widespread in the early eighteenth-century and may be seen from the works of the Englishmen Ray, Toland, Derham, Tindal and the Dutchman Nieuwentijdt, whose scientific apology for God was translated into English almost as soon as it was printed in Dutch.[2] In the early nineteenth-century William Paley (1743–1805) best exemplifies the effort. In the first half of the twentieth-century the trend was continued by William Temple (1881–1944) and Alfred North Whitehead to whom Temple was philosophically related. In America, Charles Hartshorne (1897–) and John Cobb (1926–) both of whom build on a Whiteheadian type of thinking, have joined the process.[3]

Paley's *Natural Theology* or *Evidences of the Existence and Attributes of the Deity Collected from the Appearances of Nature* published in 1802 plays the sciences for all they are worth as "proofs" of God. Like a good disciple of John Ray who, as early as 1693, classified plants and whose 1693 *Quadrupedum et Serpentini Generis* was the first classification of animals since Aristotle, Paley paraded the specifics of cosmology, entomology, botany, chemistry and especially anatomy before his reader so as to display the consummate order, design and purpose of the universe. Arguing like his predecessors, Paley was convinced and convinced his readers that each demonstration shows that the arrangement seen both in the cosmos and in living structures is to be correctly understood only as the work of an intelligent orderer, designer and purposer.

> There cannot be design without designer; contrivance without a contriver; order, without choice; arrangement, without any thing capable of arranging; subserviency and relation to a purpose, without that which could intend a purpose; means suitable to an end, and executing their office in accomplishing that end, without the end ever having been contemplated, or the means accommodated to it. Arrangement, disposition of parts, subservancy of means to an end, relation of instruments to a use, imply the presence of intelligence and mind.[4]

Paley was not satisfied with understanding the power responsible for design, order and purpose as a simple principle of efficiency, however. Rather, he was quick to note that, since the capacity to contrive or to design implies "consciousness of thought", the design itself bears evidences to the personal nature of the designer. "The acts of a mind prove the existence of mind: and in whatever a mind resides is a person." [5] Further, since every animated being has "its sensorium", that is, the space within which perception and validation are exerted, Paley, like Newton, declared that the "sensorium" of the divine being embraces the universe itself. God's ubiquity is insured by the simple device of defining God as being one with existence as such. God is thus "infinite, as well as in essence, as in power; yet nevertheless a person".[6]

As indicated above, Newtonianism, which was responsible for both the pre-Paleyan and Paleyan arguments for God derived from the concept of order and design, was idealized by Kant, whom we will have opportunity to discuss in more detail below.[7] Here the point to be noted is that, though modified and idealized, Newtonian influences continued to be responsible for the synthesis of God with the universe right up to our own time.

In the Anglo-Saxon world Kantian idealism entered theological thought with S. T. Coleridge (1772–1834) and progressed through the nineteenth-century until it reached its apex under the influence of the post-Hegelian idealism of T. H. Green (1836–1882). In America the movement was represented by Josiah Royce (1885–1916).

Process Thought

The most pertinent influences of this idealistic trend which continues into the present, is to be found in "process thought",[8] especially in the philosophy of Alfred North Whitehead. Though evidently influenced more directly by Plato than by Kant, Whitehead's attempt at a "restatement of Platonic realism"[9] is also and unavoidably an attempt to come to terms with Kant as well as his predecessors, René Descartes, John Locke (1632–1704) and David Hume (1711–1776).[10]

Temple's Theology

We begin our analysis with William Temple, whose debt to Whitehead is obvious, but whose differences are not unimportant. Temple's Gifford Lectures of 1932–1934, published under the title, *Nature, God and Man,* illustrate the situation of one entangled in the nexus of scientism, idealism, and the Christian faith. More specifically, Temple's "dialectical realism"[11] resulted from a combination of classical idealistic thought, Paleyan-type concepts and Whiteheadian process ideas in combination with biblical teachings. Like Paley's, Temple's God is "intelligence" and "mind". For Temple, however, the emphasis is upon the "immanent" God within the world rather than the "transcendent" God who designed it. God is the "immanent reason" or "logos in nature".[12] He is the life of the universe, "its informing and vitalistic principle".[13]

From the parables of Christ, Temple gathered that "in nature we find God, we do not only infer from nature what God must be like, but when we see nature truly, we see God self-manifested through it".[14] Again, as with Paley and the biblical documents, Temple insisted that God is personal. However, he was not satisfied with defining God principally as the "personal designer" of the world as was Paley. For Temple God "indwells the world, and the world is rooted in Him". God interpenetrates the creation in such a way that "the process of the world is itself the medium of His personal action".[15]

Temple's dependence on Whitehead, especially on the ideas expressed in Whitehead's *The Concept of Nature* (1920), *Science and the Modern World* (1926), *Process and Reality* (1930), and *Adventures of Ideas* (1933), is illustrative of a theology which at one and the same time is both caught in ideas of process philosophy and realizes, at least to some extent, the inherent limitations of its captor. Thus Temple's statement: "The immanent principle of the World Process is a purposive Mind, guiding the movement of electrons and of galaxies by the requirements of its unchanging purpose",[16] is definitely Whiteheadian.[17] Nevertheless, at a formal level at least, Temple refused to adopt Whitehead's completely immanent, limited, essentially non-personal concept of God who exists in interdependence with the world. In contradistinction to Whitehead's "process God" of primordial and consequent natures, who is known as he concretizes himself in reality, Temple proclaimed a God who is transcendent.[18] Rather than identify God with the world in such a way that he and the world are interdependent, Temple desired to differentiate God from the world.[19] For Temple reality is not only good, it is not only a result of God's concretizing himself, it is also evil. And God stands over against evil.[20]

In the end Temple saw the difference between the gospel and Whitehead to be so great that he came near to showing that Whitehead and the gospel are quite antithetical. Hence, while he conceded that much of what Whitehead had to say "is edifying", Temple was quick to add, "it is hard to see by what right he says it".[21] Thus, though Temple can admit, "at points" Whitehead is "very near the Christian Gospel",[22] he had some rather basic "corrections" to offer.

... if only Professor Whitehead would for "creativity" say Father, for "primordial nature of God" say Eternal Word, and for "consequent nature of God" say Holy Spirit, he would perhaps be able to show ground for his gratifying conclusions. But he cannot use those terms, precisely because each of them imports the notion of Personality as distinct from Organism. The very reason which gives to the Christian scheme its philosophic superiority is that which precludes Professor Whitehead from adopting it.[23]

Eventually, then, Temple would have no part in Whitehead's monistic optimism, his identification of God with the world, his progressively changing God or his thoroughgoing organismic conceptuality of reality which precludes conceiving of God as personal.[24]

Temple's critique was both to the point and well taken. Nevertheless, it would seem that Temple's own "Immanent Theism" was so dependent upon the same idealistically inspired epistemological concepts as those of Whitehead that the difference between the two must be considered more a matter of degree than of kind.[25] Certainly Temple's theism, which drew many of its concepts from the biblical accounts, had much more in common with what has usually been understood as being within the bounds of Christian theology than Whitehead's thought. It would seem, however, that Temple's basically stoic *deus sive natura* (God identified with nature) conceptuality was maintained along with biblical perceptions only by way of fortuitous inconsistency.

Temple's lack of decisiveness in this regard is nicely illustrated by the statement, "He is *more* and *other* than all that is in earth and heaven".[26] Though the "more" and "other" were attempts to express continuity *with* and distinction *from* nature, in the end it would seem that it was the continuity rather than the distinction which won out. Thus, the disparity which Temple would like to have between his thought and that of Whitehead finally broke down. In that Temple did allow biblical perspectives to modify his basic idealism, he was notably different from Whitehead, who simply used biblical categories to illustrate his fundamentally Platonic system. The difference, however, was not as great as one might wish for or as great as would have been the case had Temple been as jealous to maintain the biblical "distance" between God and nature as he was to show the continuity between the two.

Whitehead's God

Turning very briefly to Whitehead himself, we find Whitehead admitting that his basic conceptuality of God consisting of primordial and consequent natures[27] is the "chief exemplification" of metaphysical principles.[28] God is the "unlimited conceptual realization of the absolute wealth of potentiality",[29] and the "principle of concretion".[30] Rather than being "the foundation of the metaphysical situation",[31] he is "the ultimate limitation".[32] His existence is "the ultimate irrationality",[33] though his "nature is the ground of rationality".[34] God is named respectively "Jehovah", "Allah", "Brahma", "Father in Heaven", "Order of Heaven", "First Cause", "Supreme Being", "Chance", each name corresponding to a system of thought derived from the experiences of those who have used it.[35] Since Whitehead's conception of God was based primarily on Plato rather than the Jewish prophets, Whitehead was quite straightforward in his rejection of much of what would seem to be rather basic to the Judaeo-Christian tradition as such. The initial source of Whitehead's progressively self-and-world-completing God was not "the coercive God of the Old Testament", but Plato's God whom Whitehead thought of as "a persuasive agency". This God had manifested himself in Jesus, the lowly man from Nazareth. Jesus, who in the totality of his life disclosed "the nature of God" and was "God's agency in the world",[36] accounted for the Galilean origin of Christianity.[37] Since the life of Christ was not an exhibition of overruling power, for "its power lies in its absence of force",[38] it is here that one sees Plato's "persuasive God" manifest and propagated through the message of peace and love.

Whitehead's account of the Christian faith in *Adventures of Ideas* is notable for both its candidness and the uniqueness of its prescription. As far as Christian history itself is concerned, Whitehead's judgement is that "the period as a whole begins in barbarism and ends in failure".[39] Since Christianity has failed to eliminate the "barbaric elements" from the various manifestations of the faith, the result has been "the tragic history of Christianity".[40]

For Whitehead Christianity manifests itself in three "phases" of discovery and exemplification. The first phase as mentioned relates to "one of the greatest discoveries in the history of religion", namely, Plato's conviction near the end of his life that "the divine element in the world" is a persuasive rather than a coercive agency".[41] The second phase, which the Christian religion designates as "the supreme moment in religious history", is the life of Jesus. Since the biblical account of the life of Jesus is "fragmentary, inconsistent and uncertain", Whitehead prefers not to judge its validity. However, the "most likely tale of historic fact" contains the elements which have evoked the best in human nature. It represents "revelation in act" which "Plato divined in theory".[42]

> The Mother, the Child, and the bare manger: the lowly man, homeless and self-forgetful, with his message of peace, love and sympathy: the suffering, the agony, the tender words as life ebbed, the final despair: and the whole with the authority of supreme victory.[43]

The third phase of Christian history began with the schools of Alexandria and Antioch by theologians who, Whitehead claimed, had the distinction of being the only thinkers who, "in a fundamental metaphysical doctrine, have improved upon Plato".[44] Their accomplishment resulted in moving from a mere "icon" or idea of God in the world to knowing the third person of the Trinity as the "direct immanence of God in the world generally".[45]

For Whitehead, of course, the doctrine of direct divine immanence was a "metaphysical discovery" of first importance. However, the Fathers failed to go far enough. They excepted God from metaphysical categories, which applied to the things of the temporal world. They conceived of him under such attributes as absolute, omnipotent, omniscient source of all being. He required no relations outside of himself and was internally complete. Since Christianity had sublimated all this from "its barbaric origin"[46], the generalization was halted. "God was necessary to the World, but the World was not necessary to God."[47]

Philosophical theology, according to Whitehead, continues to have purpose nevertheless. It gives "a rational understanding of the rise of civilization". It also reminds us of "the tenderness of mere life itself in a strife-torn world".[48] In addition to this assessment, Whitehead had two practical suggestions to offer. The first was to replace the "Book of Revelation" with the "Speech of Pericles to the Athenians". The second was that the religions should learn and borrow from one another and, above all, "to learn to understand each other and love".[49]

Thus, although Temple was quite right in seeing much in Whitehead that, at least at first hearing, sounds commendable, if theology is defined by its conceptuality of God, he was also right in rejecting Whitehead's ideas as not being those which are recognizable within the Christian faith.[50] Hence, while Temple's concept of God as the immanent principle and purposive mind who guides the world process from within was also deeply Platonic, his insistence that God is complete in himself and Lord of nature led him to reject the kind of *interpenetration* between God and nature which Whitehead found necessary for his metaphysics and according to which God and nature exist in mutual dependence. Whitehead's limited, progressively self-and-world-completing God is not only the Paleyan God of design and the power within nature, he is of nature, as nature is of God. Thus, "the world lives by its incarnation of God in itself . . . . He is an actual fact in the nature of things".[51] In poetic reciprocity Whitehead expressed it again:

> It is as true to say that the World is immanent in God, as that God is immanent in the World.
> It is as true to say that God transcends the World, as that the World transcends God.
> It is as true to say that God creates the World, as that the World creates God.[52]

In sum, then, rather than being the "Creator" of the world, God himself was regarded as a part of the creative process. Thus John Cobb is surely correct when he says, "Whitehead's argument for the existence of God, insofar as there is an argument at all, is primarily the *traditional one* from the order of the universe to the ground of that order".[53]

Though the above is well taken and, while one should be somewhat cautious in challenging Cobb's understanding of Whitehead, it is questionable, at least if Cobb's statement,

"... a passionately theocentric faith may follow from the Whiteheadian vision just as appropriately as Whitehead's urbanely humanistic faith",[54] can be considered consistent with Whitehead's own thought. The fact that Whitehead never suggested that God is a living person, as Cobb knows full well,[55] is not accidental to Whitehead's system. Rather this lack of personhood was integral to Whitehead's concept of God in both God's "primordial" and "consequent" natures. In virtue of the latter God is related to "actual occasions" and in this capacity is, according to Whitehead, "an actual entity". Cobb's judgement that the description of this "actual entity" is "more like an account of a living person"[56] is thus his own.

Again, contrary to Cobb's argument, it would seem that there are more basic reasons for Whitehead's refusal to understand God as person than his understanding of persons as "temporal", as lacking "self-identity through time" and being subject to "loss of what is past" by which God cannot be qualified. By denying that these limitations are applicable to *God as person,* Cobb attempts to redefine Whitehead's God in terms of a living person and as "Creator".[57] Cobb thus tries to interpret Whitehead as Christian in spite of Whitehead himself while retaining Whitehead's philosophy largely intact.

It may, of course, be possible to know Whitehead better than Whitehead knew himself. One is reminded of the rabbinic story that Rabbi Akiba understood what God said to Moses on Mount Sinai better than did Moses. However, if one follows Whitehead's order of thought from the world to God and thinks of God not as transcendent Creator[58] but as the result of the creative process, then to rebaptize God as a personal Creator would seem somewhat difficult. Cobb admits that Whitehead used language about God univocally and not analogically;[59] hence, his terms about creation referred with equal force to God. Therefore, even in the case of "God", "Hume's principle of derivation of conceptual experience from physical experience remains without any exception".[60] Thus, according to Whitehead, God remains very much of creation. God may be a higher, perhaps even a person-like order of creation, but he is certainly not a person who is quite other than the world, one who created it and interacts with other persons in it.

In sum, if we understand Whitehead, as Whitehead is surely to be understood, it would be difficult to put a Christian halo on him. It may be possible to place him among the saints who represent Indian or Chinese thought, as Whitehead himself suggested,[61] or among those of Buddhism as Hartshorne indicates,[62] but hardly among those venerated by the Judaeo-Christian tradition.

Here Temple's "dialectical realism", illogical as it would sometimes appear to be,[63] which made use of Whitehead's thought while ultimately rejecting his concept of God, would nevertheless seem to be more consequential than current process theology which Cobb represents.[64] Cobb, of course, is quite cognizant of Temple's critique of Whitehead as he is also aware of Stephen Ely's negative conclusion as to "the religious availability" of Whitehead's God.[65] So attractive is Whitehead's process thought to Cobb, however, that he seems first to modify Whitehead's philosophy so as to be able to import the Christian concept of God as a person and as creator into it and then to modify that concept with the Whiteheadian categories of limitation and creativity. Hence, neither for Cobb nor for Whitehead is God the transcendent personal Creator who creates *ex nihilo* and whose creation is substantially separate from but contingent upon him. In sum, Cobb would bring the Judaeo-Christian concept of God into Whitehead's system only insofar as the philosophy of process is able to welcome it.

Hartshorne's Theism

Charles Hartshorne, to whom Cobb owes his understanding and love of Whitehead, develops his own theology of process, a "neo-classic theism" which represents a continuing development in what might be called the "idealistic Whiteheadian mood". Though Hartshorne's natural theology in its genesis is based on Royce rather than Whitehead, his ideas identify with those of Whitehead to the degree that he is quite candid in admitting that his theological conceptions are most at home in a philosophy of the Buddhist-Whiteheadian type.[66] For Hartshorne, God is the wholeness of the world, correlative to the wholeness of every sound individual dealing with the world.[67] This *divine reality* which results from Hartshorne's "creationist or neo-classical metaphysics" [68] not only includes "all contingent things", but, like the rest of actuality, it is itself contingent. It is the "supreme process". Lesser realities are "instances of an inferior form of process".[69] God is both finite and infinite and likewise both relative and absolute, conditioned and unconditioned, mutable and immutable, contingent and necessary.[70] He is both *cause* and *caused*.[71] As cause he is the "concrete cause of each event". As caused, he is the "effect of prior events, including prior divine events or experiences".[72] In that creation and humanity are included in this "eventness", "we are not simply co-creators with God of the world, but in the last analysis co-creators, with him, of himself".[73]

Since Hartshorne's God, like Whitehead's, is integral to nature itself, he is as finite or infinite as nature is finite or infinite, as creative nature is creative, as created as nature is created, as immanent within nature as nature is immanent within him. For Hartshorne, then, as for Whitehead, it would seem that in the end God is a part of nature rather than a God who transcends nature. Instead of being the sovereign Creator of creation, God is as much *of* creation as creation is *of* God. If this judgement is correct, Whitehead's and Hartshorne's and even Cobb's "God" would seem to be subject to the same kind of criticism as any other *deus sive natura* theistic notion except that an additional factor has to be included, namely, the penetration of God by nature. This "all-in-God" doctrine is a revival of the mid-nineteenth-century "panentheism" of K. C. F. Krause by which Krause attempted to reconcile theism and pantheism with the subjectivism of Kant and Fichte and the absolutism of Schelling and Hegel.[74]

Epistemologically speaking, since as Whitehead candidly admits, God is the exemplification of metaphysical principles,[75] God would seem to be simply a necessary aspect of finite reality by which reality is explained and brought to cognitive completion. His "godness" has to do with his ubiquity and creative power within creation rather than his transcendent power over and responsibility for creation as such.

Thus "God" is the answer to a metaphysical quest rather than the one upon whom the whole of creation including its metaphysical aspects is dependent. Whitehead's concept of

God, then, on which the whole of process theology would seem to rely is part and parcel of his general system of metaphysics which begins with individual experience of reality based on "direct knowledge of the world as a datum for the immediacy of feeling",[76] and completes itself in thought structures considered necessary for the occurrence of this experience. Understood from the point of view of epistemology, Whitehead then would simply seem to be a more modern but less specifically Christian rendition of Schleiermacher, for whom doctrine was a matter of "feeling coming to rest in thought".[77] As Cobb puts it:

> It would be best to say that he [Whitehead] began with human experience *as we know it* and as we further understand it in the light of science, and then presented the question as to what must be the case in order that this experience can occur.[78]

An interesting contrast is apparent when we compare Whitehead's, and by implication Hartshorne's, concepts of God with that of another mathematician and philosopher Blaise Pascal (1623–1662). "The God of the philosophers" which Pascal rejected is here recreated. "The God of Abraham, Isaac and Jacob" whom Pascal along with Judaeo-Christian tradition in general confesses is considered outmoded.[79] From this perspective, as Weizsäcker reminds us, Pascal was wiser than the philosophers. When he came to the conclusion that God was not to be found in mathematics, he gave it up and "sought God where he could be found".[80]

Whitehead Meets Einstein

Another way of looking at the matter, as far as the development of science is concerned, is to remind ourselves of the relationship of Whiteheadian thought to modern science. As pointed out, Whitehead's, Hartshorne's and, even to a certain extent, Temple's ideas of God and theology are, somewhat directly, the result of the seventeenth and eighteenth-centuries' scientific development. However, as is quite obvious from the history of the development of modern science, it is exactly this "God of the philosophers", this *deus sive natura,* inter-penetrating-nature-kind of God which, in its Platonic-Augustinian forms, as well as in its Aristotelian-Thomistic articulations, *had to be overcome* before science, as we know it, could be developed in the first place.[81]

In that Whitehead is one of the first philosophers who has attempted to construct a post-Einsteinian system, and in view of the fact that his "process philosophy" continues to have influence in theological thought, especially in America, it may be well to devote some little space to comparing Whitehead's conceptual basis with that of modern science. Whitehead at one and the same time adopts Albert Einstein's (1879–1955) concept of relational space but disagrees with his interpretation of it.[82] Nevertheless it would seem that the adequacy of Whitehead's system, and hence the adequacy of any theological concepts based upon it, will depend on how well Whitehead's procedures and claims fare in comparison with those of Einstein in particular whose thought in many ways is paradigmatic for epistemology as a whole.

In attempting to overcome one of the oldest and thorniest problems of scientific thought which Whitehead terms the "bifurcation of nature",[83] i.e., the difference between nature *as we experience it* and nature *according to scientific definition*, Whitehead insisted that nature is given to us as immediate awareness. Hence, though at one point he defined nature in terms of the deliverance of sense awareness,[84] he did so only to show that such a definition was too restrictive to define reality as a whole. Thus, he would agree with the Ionian philosopher Democritus (*c.* 460–*c.* 370 B.C.), for instance, who insisted that that which we sense gives only confused knowledge because the senses indicate only how things affect us and that in a rather superficial way. Hence, for Whitehead the way reality presents itself to us in immediacy is much more complicated than a simple dependence on sense data or "sensa" as he calls them.[85] Since sense perception does not provide the data in terms of which to interpret it and since a myriad of factors enter into the way we see, hear, etc., Whitehead's understanding of sense perception is akin to Hume's "hybred character of our perceptions" and was tacitly presupposed by Locke as well.[86] Nevertheless, the fact that Whitehead thought of nature as being known or *prehended* in *presentational immediacy* would seem to make his system dependent upon some kind of *one to one relationship* between the presentation of nature to the individual and nature as it actually is. If so, it falls into the same kind of epistemological difficulty as the pre-Humean, Newtonian dependence upon sensible phenomena although in Whitehead's case, it is the intuition which is involved.[87]

The history of science from Copernicus, Galileo and Newton onwards has made it clear, as Whitehead knows, that, far from being obvious or a matter of immediate awareness, there is often a profound difference between our experience of an object and the object as it is understood by science.[88] Scientific knowledge results from probing into and making propositions about reality which need testing simply because reality is often different from the way we apprehend it and because our actual experience of reality, as it presents itself to us, often affords us only signals to reality which must be deciphered if they are to be understood. Reality itself may or may not reveal itself to our experience, depending on how we have been "schooled" to experience. Thus, the earth revolves around the sun and rotates on its axis in spite of the fact that we are never *immediately* aware of and never experience it doing so. By and large, the universe continues to present itself *immediately* to us as it did to Ptolemy, which is exactly the reason why the Ptolemaic system lasted as long as it did. We are never aware of the fact, for instance, that when we stand upright our heads are pointed in one direction with regard to the universe at 12.00 o'clock noon and in nearly the opposite direction at 12.00 o'clock midnight. Or again, space and time *present themselves* to us as separate entities. Space seems boundless and time endless. Relativity physics, however, indicates that there is only space-time and space-time is finite. The difference between immediate awareness and actuality is especially acute in micro-physics, the realities of which are realized only through "secondary phenomena" — clicks of a geiger-counter, tracks in a bubble chamber, or blips on a screen. As Whitehead knows, it is only by the mental process of systemizing the clicks, tracks and blips into a consistent pattern, by deciphering the code, if you will, that we understand that these "secondary phenomena" correspond to realities which are beyond the threshold of immediate awareness.[89] Whitehead's attempt to de-emphasize conceptual experience, and center our direct apprehension of the world around us in the emotions, would seem to place him in a position where he would have extreme difficulty in dealing with the world as we know it.

In particular, as F. S. C. Northrop (1893–   ) has pointed out, Whitehead's inability to deal with Einstein's denial of universal simultaneity shows the weakness of Whitehead's system and hence of his basic epistemology which depends upon immediate individual awareness as such.[90] We may, for instance, be presented with two separated events as happening at the same time, i.e., *simultaneously.* However, since as Einstein has shown, factors such as (1) the distance from the events to the observer, (2) the possibility that the events and the observer may be in separate coordinate systems in either uniform or non-uniform motion, and (3) the fact that events which appear simultaneous to an observer in one coordinate system may not appear simultaneous to an observer in another system, rule out universal simultaneity.

I may very well have an *impression,* or to use Whitehead's terms, undergo "a process of presentational immediacy" of the simultaneity of spatially separated events in a "nexus, the regions of which are defined by the "sensa",[91] such as seeing two lightning flashes or hearing two thunderclaps at the same time. However, the question of when the lightning flashes or thunderclaps actually occurred, at what time they took place, can only be ascertained by way of complicated calculation. To use Whitehead's terminology, if a bolt of lightning were to strike very near where I am standing, I would *prehend* the flash and *be presented with* the ensuing thunder almost immediately. An observer some miles distant would *experience* the flash shortly after I had and *be made immediately aware* of the thunder-clap a good deal later. The explanation is simple enough. Light travels much faster than sound. The example is relevant in two ways. On the one hand, it shows that any correlation which one makes between an immediate impression and the reality signified by the presented data is necessarily a matter of calculation. On the other hand, since universal simultaneity is ruled out, universal time is ruled out as well.

The result is that Whitehead's correlation of "conscious perception"[92] with *event* along with his and Hartshorne's concept of "a process-becoming God", who depends upon an exact differentiation between past and future, a differentiation which is annulled when universal time is ruled out, are both quite out of the question. Rather than taking Einsteinian relativity as defining reality, therefore, Whitehead's and Hartshorne's epistemological systems and their "knowledge of God" continue to be dependent on relationships with reality of a kind which Einstein has shown no longer obtain.[93]

Thus, when Hartshorne discerns that, according to relativity physics, there is no "definite cosmic present" (i.e., no definite simultaneity)[94] and that the theory of relativity denies any possible "right frame of reference for the cut between the past and the future",[95] his answer is a rather weak: "Somehow relativity as an *observational truth* (sic) must be compatible with divine unsurpassability".[96]

Hartshorne's further speculation regarding "suprarelative simultaneity" which the cosmic observer might discern[97] compounds the problem in a two-fold way. In the first place, the "cosmic observer" would seem to have to "sit" outside the process of the cosmos. Such a "cosmic observer" may well come closer to reflecting the God of Abraham, Isaac and Jacob than does the God of process philosophy who is bound up with the cosmos. He would seem to be rather a contradiction, however, to both Hartshorne's and Whitehead's God who exists in interdependence with the world. Secondly, since Whitehead's and Hartshorne's "God" is tied into the historical process, he would have some little difficulty, to say the least, in coping with a cosmos wherein space-time relationships are dependent upon velocity and gravity as in Einsteinian physics.[98] In "Einstein's universe", history is as variant as are the velocity and gravitational relationships of "the worlds" in relation to which these histories take place. The fact that even on earth, and as observed from sea level, a clock at high altitudes ticks more quickly than a "sychronized" one at sea level, and one in a fast flying airplane when observed from a "stationary position" on earth ticks more slowly than a "stationary" one on the ground ought to make anyone pause who tries to conceive of a universal God who is dependent upon time and historical processes as such.

Thus, though Whitehead has made a valiant attempt to unify nature and to show that knowledge, instead of being a matter of simple subject-object differentiation, comprises a relationship of inner subjectivity, the price of his doing away with the distinction between "nature as sensed and nature as designated by scientific theory" [99] is that he was quite unable to account for it in accordance with the way experimental science is actually pursued. Taken to its logical conclusion, Whitehead's theory ends in pure solipsism. As Northrop, with reference to Einstein, has pointed out, unless we respect the differentiation between our individual impressions of an event and our designation of that event by postulated public physical definition, i.e., by scientific theory, there is no way in which two observers could speak about the same event at all.[100] In that case, there could be no public knowledge whatsoever.

The fact that, when confronting the problem of what may be called "misperception", Whitehead hedged his bets is interesting to say the least. As guarantees of the correctness of conscious perception, he cited Hume's test of "force and vivacity" (shades of Descartes), and added to this "the illumination by consciousness of the various feelings involved in the "process". However, "neither of these tests is infallible". Thus a third had to be offered. "There is also the delayed test, that the future conforms to expectations derived from this assumption." [101] However, in that there is no hint and indeed no possibility of future confirmation of the correctness of a conscious perception within the "process of presentational immediacy" by which "actual entities" or "actual occasions" [102] present themselves, it would seem that Whitehead's third and indeed, from our point of view, necessary "guarantee" undercuts his epistemological position as a whole.

In the end, then, Whitehead's attempt to deal with the dualism, which he sees between nature as immediately presented to the individual and nature as designated by scientific theory, left no grounds for either agreement or disagreement between individuals about reality. Whitehead's "prehended" universe[103] depends purely on the individual involved as "the subject which is prehending".[104] Not only does this overload individual experience of reality, i.e., attribute to it much more than it is able to deliver, but it gives rise to a system which in surrendering itself to the individual's "immediate awareness" cannot account for public reality at all. In the end, reality is, then, surely a matter of personal arbitrariness. Thus, it is not coincidental that Whitehead could quote William James (1842–1910):

> Your acquaintance with reality grows literally by buds or drops of perception. Intellectually and on reflection you can divide these into components, but as immediately given, they come totally or not at all.[105]

Even more telling is Whitehead's statement, "Just as Descartes said, 'this body is mine'; so he should have said, 'this actual world is mine'".[106]

An incident with Einstein, reported by Northrop, is both interesting and illustrative in this regard. After Einstein had confessed that he simply did not understand Whitehead, Northrop explained that Whitehead evolved his theory of a single continuum of events by seeking to avoid the bifurcation between phenomenal events and "the postulated physically defined public events".

> Einstein replied, "Oh! Is that what he means? That would be wonderful! So many problems would be solved were it true! Unfortunately, it is a fairy tale. Our world is not as simple as that". After a moment's silent reflection, he added "On that theory there would be no meaning to two observers speaking about the same event".[107]

In spite of the criticisms offered above, it would be wrong to judge the efforts of those who have tried to come to terms with science as being entirely negative. If we remember, as Günter Howe insists, that all theological discourse is bound to use the concepts of contemporary thought, then Paley, Temple, Whitehead and Hartshorne and, following the latter two, Cobb, may well be commended for their overt attempts to come to terms with the scientifically-influenced thought structures of their own times.[108]

What they have done, however, shows that in such attempts it is extraordinarily easy for "contemporary thought" so to modify the terms of the Judaeo-Christian tradition that continuity is easily lost and theology simply becomes the projection of "the good", "the beautiful", "the necessary", "the immanent", "the process", or whatever some system of contemporary thought would seem to demand. Unless we are extremely circumspect, such endeavors will lead us so to subject God to our understanding of the universe that, rather than speaking of him, we speak only of ourselves. Hence we would be justly accused by the dictum that, though in the beginning God created us, we now put ourselves in the position of returning the compliment.

To reiterate, the problem of using contemporary concepts rightly to explicate theology is an extremely complicated and delicate one. Unless the theologian is very careful, the utilization of contemporary thought forms in terms of their "everyday content" to explain the content of theology can easily result in subordinating theology to thought structures that are so alien to it that in the end they quite distort it. Hence, instead of theology *informing* "contemporary thought", or utilizing contemporary thought forms to explicate its content, contemporary thought *forms* theology. The end result is one kind of *Kulturchristentum* (culture Christianity) or another and theology becomes a prisoner of the very forces to which it attempts to show the way of freedom and truth. On the other hand, the temptation to leave things as they are and thus continue the *status quo* in the hope that the ancient message will somehow make itself relevant to the modern world is to fly in the face of our knowledge of epistemological developments in general and those appertaining to natural science in particular.

Whether we like it or not, thought structures change through history. Hence, to repeat the same message in the same words is very likely to state a different message. Also, whether we like it or not, past theological concepts are somewhat culturally dependent. They have been conditioned by the concepts of the cultures in which theology has developed. Thus it should not surprise us that biblical-critical studies have uncovered divergent conceptualities within the biblical documents themselves. The philosophical concepts of the Hellenistic culture had more than a little influence on the formulation of doctrine in the formative period of the Church. The gist of the matter is that, as theology has necessarily made use of certain concepts of past cultures in order to explicate its content in places where that culture dominated, so it must consider the natural scientific habit of mind which greatly influences our thought patterns today. Only by recognizing the inevitable influence of cultural concepts on theological discourse will

theology be circumspect enough to avoid the pitfalls of sub-
servience to culture, on the one hand, and irrelevance to it, on
the other.

Continental Newtonianism

On the continent of Europe the argument based on Newtonian
physics had considerably less direct impact on shaping theological thought than in Britain. It is true, of course, that English
Deism, which took full advantage of Newtonian physics to
promote its designer concept of Deity read off the pattern of
the universe, spilled over onto the continent to influence both
François Voltaire (1694–1778) and Jean-Jacques Rousseau
(1712–1778). In Germany Johann Albert Fabricius
(1688–1736) gathered a "physio-theological" circle around
himself to discuss the theological value of astronomy, biology,
chemistry and physics. As far as theology is concerned, the
most important result of Fabricius' effort was its effect upon
his son-in-law, Herrmann Samuel Reimarus (1694–1768).
Reimarus was to become responsible for bringing the deistic
point of view into German intellectual circles with his explosive
*Apologie oder Schutzschrift für die vernünftigen Verehrer
Gottes (Apology for the Reasonable Worshippers of God).*
Reimarus had written the 4000 page document over a period
of some twenty years between 1745 and 1765 and for fear of
reprisals distributed it only among a few friends. Having "discovered" the writing in the Wolfenbüttel library of which he
was curator, Gottwald Ephraim Lessing (1729–1781)
published it in part as *Fragmente eines Ungenannten (Anonym-
ous Fragments)* between 1774 and 1778. The writings were a
trenchant critique of the Christian faith from a rationalist point
of view which, radical as they were, or perhaps because they
were radical, at least introduced the culture of the day to the
possibility of differentiating between the faith as it had
developed and its original sources. Many of Reimarus' conclusions may be considered to depend more on imagination than
evidence. Thus Jesus' walking on the water is explained as his
walking on the shore in the fog, and it is alleged that the
disciples having discovered that preaching was preferable to
fishing invented the tale of the resurrection so as to be able to

continue their mission. However the document anticipated a good deal of later critical thought in the investigation of Scripture.

Nevertheless, on the continent there was on the whole little attempt to make theological capital out of linking the order of the universe as apprehended by Newtonian science to the concept of a universal designer such as one finds in British post-Newtonians from Ray to Paley. Likewise, as far as "mainline theology" was concerned, there was little attempt to identify God with metaphysical concepts of nature in the way of Whitehead, Temple or Hartshorne. This does not mean that Newtonian classical physics simply passed theology by. Rather, as mentioned above, in German-speaking Europe, which has been the cradle for much of our theological thought from the beginning of the eighteenth-century onward, Newtonianism came into the main stream of theology by the back door, as it were, through Immanuel Kant. Thus Kant's thought, one way or another, became foundational for Protestant theological thinking from Friedrich Schleiermacher and Albrecht Ritschl down to Adolph von Harnack. So pervasive is Kant that even Karl Barth, who rightly protested against the Kantian anthropocentric subjectivization of nineteenth-century theology, is not entirely free of his influence.

Kant's Transcendentalism

Kant began his university studies in theology but was soon attracted to mathematics and physics. He became an early devotee of Newton and wrote treatises on the causes of earthquakes, the nature of winds and the general theory of the heavens. His "nebular hypothesis" which explained the galaxies as spiral disks like our own Milky Way and his thesis that the apparent variation in velocity of celestial phenomena over the years is due to the minute deceleration of the earth's rotation, resulting from tidal friction caused by the moon, still command respect. Hence, it is not surprising to learn that Kant lectured on science and mathematics as well as philosophy for fifteen years at the University of Königsberg before becoming Professor of Philosophy in 1720.

Scientist as he was, and because he was a scientific thinker,

Kant was shocked into writing his *Critiques,* the philosophy by which he is known, by the thought of Scottish philosopher David Hume as expressed in the latter's *Treatise on Human Nature.* In the treatise Hume questioned the validity of the universal principle of causality upon which the whole of the scientific enterprise depended. Having inherited his empiricism from Locke, Hume pressed Locke's conclusions — that we only know reality as a result of the impressions of things given to our senses and our reflections upon them — to its logical conclusion and ended up in a thoroughgoing scepticism.

The gist of the problem goes back to Descartes. Descartes, as we have seen, in his search for certainty operated with a bifurcation between mind and matter and used God to correlate the two. Newton, who was as credulous as Descartes in believing both that mathematics was the certain way of truth and that God designed the universe in such a way that we could know it as it is, continued to operate with Descartes' separation between mind and reality. Like Descartes, Newton had not the slightest doubt that the mind could automatically read the truth off the world's phenomena as they were presented to it.

For Locke, who provided the direct basis for Hume, as for most of us, the fact that reality is correlated with apprehension was simply a matter of "common sense". I know the chair is a chair because it presents itself to my mind as a chair and presents itself to everyone else in the same way. Hence we know reality in common. "It may be so", said Hume and I believe it too, but since all reality must be perceived reality and it is not possible to perceive any relationship between sense perception and phenomena, such a belief is merely a matter of convention. More particularly, since it is not possible to observe the relationship between an event and its antecedent, the assumption of universal cause and effect, which is the basis of all science, particularly of the Newtonian physics, as well as all ordinary perception, is called into question. That being the case, there is no way to prove that the phenomena we perceive are objectively real or that our knowledge of the world is true.

It was this argument which induced Kant to write in his *Prolegomena to Any Future Metaphysic:*

> I honestly confess, the suggestion of David Hume was the very thing which many years ago first interrupted my dogmatic

slumber, and gave my investigations in the field of speculative philosophy a new direction.[109]

Causality, for Hume, was "a convention without proof". It was founded on "inference",[110] based on "custom", "habit",[111] and the supposition that "the future will be conformable to the past".[112] In the light of Hume's (from my point of view, justified) scepticism which called both Newtonian science (which, for Kant, was the touchstone of truth), and with it the whole epistemological enterprise, as then understood, into question, Kant set out to write a critical metaphysics which would justify knowledge "on the secure path of science".[113] His first step was to separate the mode of cognition of objects from the objects themselves. He then conceived and systematized the laws necessary for both perception and understanding into a "transcendental philosophy" according to which the world would again make sense.[114]

Although the attempt would hardly have impressed Hume, since his critique of the cause and effect relationship called even the *phenomena* with which it dealt into question, there is no belying the magnificence of Kant's effort. Whereas, for Locke, whose empiricism ended in Hume's scepticism, mind was a passive *tabula rasa* which simply absorbed the impressions of the world as delivered to it by the senses in experience, for Kant, the mind itself contributed to perception in the acts of experience. Hume was quite right, as Kant saw it, in rejecting the common sense belief that there was any observable proof of knowledge or of phenomena. Experience, Kant saw, was a matter of making judgements differentiating one thing from another. There are "analytic judgements", judgements in which the predicate is integral to the subject, e.g., "This body is extended". A judgement of this kind is not a matter of knowledge but of definition. Then there are "synthetic judgements" which if true qualify as knowledge. These are judgements which add a predicate to a subject such as, "This body is heavy". At the same time it is quite evident that synthetic judgements are not obvious, e.g., the judgement that an object is "heavy" is not *ipso facto* based upon experience. Hence, synthetic judgements which are necessary to knowledge involve non-experiential factors. Locke's empiricism in which knowledge is simply a matter of sense impression is thus ruled out.[115]

Synthetic judgements are necessary to be sure because without them the world would not make sense. The world, especially as defined by Newtonian physics did as a matter of fact make sense. Of this Kant was never in doubt any more than Descartes was in doubt of mathematics or Newton was in doubt of his law of gravity which applied to the behavior of the solar system. Having been jarred by Hume, Kant realized that phenomena as grasped by the senses could neither be the source of sense experience nor be considered as reality itself (*das Ding an sich*). They merely represented reality to the senses. At the same time Kant, like Hume, was quite unwilling to grasp at God like Descartes and Bishop Berkeley (1685–1753) in order to hook mind and reality together. Hence, for Kant, the only possible source for the constructive categories necessary to experience had to be *the mind* or *the understanding* itself. Since these categories cannot be *a posteriori*, i.e., after experience, they must be *a priori*, i.e., prior to experience. Hence Kant's statement: "The understanding does not draw its laws (*a posteriori*) from nature but prescribes them (*a priori*) and its prescriptions determine the way nature shows itself to us".[116]

To repeat, since Hume had demonstrated that the knowledge of all phenomena was a matter of convention and hence was subjective and arbitrary, Kant proposed to correlate subjectivity and objectivity by insisting that the subjective conditions which make knowledge possible set the rules by which phenomena are known. His basic move was to transfer Newton's space and time from the world of phenomena where they could be questioned to the realm of the *a priori* where they became the absolute categories of apprehension, the pure forms of sensibility. It is, then, under the *a priori* categories of space and time that phenomena are perceived. In addition, the categories of *causality* and *substance* conform phenomena to the understanding so that they have the possibility of being experienced. Thus, there is direct correlation between that which makes experience possible and that which makes nature possible.

> The possibility of experience in general is therefore at the same time the universal law of nature, and the principles of the former [experience] are the very laws of the latter [nature].[117]

For Hume, then, *cause and effect* are matters of customary conjunction between sequential events; they are matters of belief rather than of proof. Any acknowledgement of *fact* or recognition of *existence* is derived from some object which is present to the memory or to the senses. Ascertaining reality is a matter of *customary conjunction* between an object remembered or sensed and some other object.[118] For Kant, phenomena are things as they appear to us, i.e., they are perceived and known insofar as they "fit" or conform to the structures of mind. That which is, then, properly perceived as phenomenon is *ipso facto* representative of reality insofar as we are able to know reality at all. It is *true* if one desires to use the term. According to Hume, one may *believe* in cause and effect relationships and one conventionally does. Reality may, in fact, conform to such belief and "be true", but it cannot be proven; it is simply *co-terminous with "natural belief"*. The difference between Hume and Kant at this point is that, whereas Hume could admit to a possible arbitrariness in the apprehension of reality, Kant attempted to elevate the concepts of mind, by which such apprehensions take place, to an objective status. However, while the mind is held to apprehend the objects of experience (i.e., phenomena) it is thought to apprehend them only insofar as it conforms them to itself.

> . . . the highest legislation of nature must lie in ourselves (that is, in our understanding), and that we must not seek the universal laws of nature in nature by means of experience, but conversely must seek nature, as to its universal conformity to law, in the conditions of the possibility of experience, which lie in our sensibility and in our understanding.[119]

Space and time, then, are "pure *a priori*" intuitions (hence not subject to doubt) which correspond to "concepts" and can be united synthetically with them.[120] Objects, i.e., phenomena, though not known "in themselves", are knowable insofar as they can be apprehended via the intuition under the categories of "space" and "time". Knowledge of actual reality or "empirical knowledge" is brought about by a correlation through *intuition* of empirical percepts with the *concepts of understanding*. This uniting or *synthesization* takes place in the transcendental, i.e., non-phenomenological, act of apperception.

How is nature at all possible in the *material* sense, as to intuition,

[I mean nature] considered as the complex of phenomena; how are space, time, and that which fills both — the object of sensation, in general possible? The answer is: By means of the constitution of our Sensibility, according to which it is specifically affected by objects, which are in themselves unknown to it, and totally distinct from those phenomena. . . . How is nature possible in the formal sense, nature as the complex of the rules, under which all phenomena must come, in order to be thought as connected in experience? The answer must be this: It is only possible by means of the constitution of our Understanding, according to which all the above representations of the sensibility are necessarily referred to a consciousness, and by which the peculiar way in which we think (that is, by rules), and hence experience also, are possible . . .[121]

Hume's challenge to "causality" was answered, therefore, by way of Kant's "synthetic unity of apperception" which is itself *a priori* and hence assured the "law of causality". Perceptions unified in cause and effect nexus according to "the law of causality" result in *experience* which, for Kant, is simply "the empirical cognition of phenomena".[122] A last citation from Kant which insures both universality and objectivity, sums up the matter:

. . . as time contains the sensuous condition *a priori* of the possibility of a continuous progression of that which exists to that which follows it, the understanding, by virtue of the unity of apperception, contains the condition *a priori* of the possibility of a continuous determination of the position in time of all phenomena, and this by means of the series of causes and effects, the former of which necessitates the sequence of the latter, and thereby renders universally and for all time, and by consequence, objectively valid, the empirical cognition of the relations of time.[123]

By making the mind responsible for both the "intuitions of reality" and the "concepts of understanding" which, via proper synthesis, the mind perceives and constitutes reality, Kant put humankind in the center of the universe as surely as Nicholas Copernicus (1473–1543) put the sun in the center of the solar system. Thus, the Kantian subjective "Copernican revolution" is a reversal of the Copernican cosmological one.

By putting the self with its understanding in the center of the universe (for it was the self which made out the diversity of impressions a unity, and hence made the "universe"), Kant's "Copernican revolution in philosophy" turned the Newtonian world inside out. Rather than reality impressing itself upon a passive mind as in the thought of Descartes and Locke, the mind impressed its rules of understanding upon passive reality. The world again made sense or so it seemed. At any rate, Kant's "critical philosophy" soon spread to every German-speaking university and students flocked to Königsberg perpetuating a wave of thought that still laps at the shores of our minds.

There would seem little doubt about the fact that in attributing to mind an active part in the knowing process, Kant's contribution to epistemology is invaluable. There would also seem to be little doubt however that the absolutization of his system, which completely subjects reality to the knowing mind, began a process of individual subjectivism in philosophy, and, as it happened, in theology, which we have yet to overcome. With Kant the Cartesian rejection of the heteronomy of authority, which subjected the self to external authority, reached finality with the autonomy of the self, subjugating reality to it. It seemed never to have occurred to Kant, as indeed it never occurred to Descartes, that different minds with equally legitimate credentials would or could picture the world in different ways any more than it occurred to Newton, on whose physics Kant built his "metaphysics", that his concept of the universe might be one of many.

An analogy may help us see the importance of this. There seems to be no question that it was the pervasiveness and persuasiveness of the philosophies of Plato and Aristotle which caused Ptolemy (*c.* 90–160 A.D.) to turn his back on the heliocentric theory which Aristarchus of Samos (*c.* 270 B.C.) had proclaimed in the third-century B.C. As a result, Ptolemy's re-establishment of the geocentric system in the face of Aristarchus' heliocentrism held back the development of cosmology some 1,500 years. In the same way, to some extent at least, we suffer the effects of the primacy of subjectivity which results from Kant's absolute "Ptolemaic type" of epistemology. What the earth had lost in being deprived of its central status of the universe in Copernicus' heliocentric cosmology, Kant restored to humankind in his human-mind-centered epistemology with such exclusive vengeance that the world's *Geistesgeschichte* (intellectual history), including theology, continues to be affected today.

Though Kant intended to universalize and objectivize knowledge – and in doing so, it must be admitted, he broke the hold of the logic of deduction ("dogmatism" as he referred to it) and pointed to a place for the subjective element in any knowledge process — in the end his categories serve to individualize and subjectivize the apprehension of reality to a degree that can only be considered detrimental. This new emphasis on the individualistic subjectivization of reality via the "categories of understanding" which Kant intended to be an advance on the "innate ideas" of Descartes and Gottfried von Leibniz (1646–1716) was directly instrumental in setting the mood for the self-oriented "neo-Protestant theology" on the Continent and not only on the Continent but in Britain and eventually in America as well.[124]

Thus, as Karl Barth has put it, no one represents the "mature man" of the Enlightenment, man emerged from his "self-inflicted state of minority", man responsible for himself and man constituted by his autonomous reason which, in turn, constitutes the world in the way that Kant does.[125] Since Kant put the individual at the center of his universe and made him responsible for it, the watchword of the Enlightenment, as Barth pointed out, is Kant's *sapere aude,* "Have the courage to make use of your own understanding".[126]

Kant's discussion of religion, though somewhat ancillary to our primary epistemological concern, is of interest insofar as it furthered the Cartesian dichotomy between faith, on the one hand, and scientific knowledge, on the other. In his *Religion innerhalb der Grenzen der blossen Vernunft (Religion Within the Limits of Reason Alone),* Kant placed matters of faith wholly within the realm of the transcendent. The categories of religion were held to be non-phenomenological. Hence, they are *ipso facto* outside the realm of experience. Thus, God, freedom and immortality are assumptions. They are as necessary for morality as the *a priori* categories of the understanding are necessary for the apprehension of nature. Along with the "categorical imperative", that universal feeling of *oughtness,* which makes moral judgements possible, because "I ought" implies "I can",

God, freedom and immortality are certain because without them life would be ambiguous at best and meaningless at worst. Kant is also certain, however, that, like the *noumena* (things in themselves), they are not subject to knowledge. One may know there is a God, for instance, but because he is not intuitable under the categories of space and time, one cannot *know* him. The result, as in Descartes' thought, is that scientific knowledge is one thing, religious faith quite another. The former has relevance for the world, the latter only for the self. Since each is confined to its own separate realm, the two are neither united nor in conflict; thus science goes one way and theology the other.

Hegel's Idealism

It is exactly at the juncture of this "unacceptable dualism" that Georg Wilhelm Friedrich Hegel (1770–1831) began his task of attempting to show *the self-development of the rational with the world process* in which process the development of the individual as such, rather than being separate from reality, was included as a member of the whole.[127] Hegel was influenced by both J. G. Fichte's (1762–1814) appreciation of science and F. W. J. von Schelling's (1775–1854) transcendentalism. In the end, however, Fichte's *Ich ist Alles* ("The self is everything") principle, which is Fichte's attempt to express the *ego* as infinite and all-encompassing, subjectivized his thought to a degree which Hegel could not bear. Fichte's stress on the noumenal aspect of nature along with his identification of the self with the absolute tended to reduce phenomena to appearances. It thus became the mere negative pole of the one all-pervading spirit. The *ego* was set over against the *non-ego* of nature and reality was to be found only in the subject, i.e., the self.[128]

Likewise, as far as Hegel is concerned, Schelling's transcendentalism eventually proved unsatisfactory. In Schelling's *Alles ist Ich* ("Everything is the self"), it is the "unity", the one infinite substance, the one absolute which displays itself as either spirit or nature with equal equanimity in an organismic whole. The dynamic of this continuing dénouement eventuated in a process which contained within itself its own contradiction.

The contradiction, in turn, propelled the process forward in a perpetual series of disclosures. The whole is apprehended not by reason, which is both a part of the process and in any case was, for Schelling, too easily identified with the spirit and the subjective idealism of Fichte, but directly by intuition.[129] Hegel was too much of a scientist to accept Fichte's Platonic-like non-reality of nature — nature as a mere shadow of the reality which was spirit — as he was too much of an absolutist to consign reality to Fichte's *ego*. Likewise, he was too much of a Kantian idealist to accept Schelling's identification of spirit and nature. For Hegel, as for Kant, "The absolute is not substance but subject".[130]

More than coincidence marks the fact that Hegel, like Kant, began his studies in theology. Like Kant, too, Hegel was a Newtonian scientist. He wrote his qualifying dissertation for becoming a *Privatdozent* (instructor) at the University of Jena, entitling it "On the Orbits of Planets". Also, like Kant, he lectured on mathematics as well as philosophy. However, whereas Kant distinguished between the *phenomena* about which knowledge could be gained, the *noumena* which underlay the phenomena but *ipso facto* could not be known, and the categories of understanding by which the knowledge of phenomena was made possible, Hegel was concerned to discern the essence of the totality of reality. This essence, "this substance of the universe", is reason (divine wisdom, God, Spirit, idea) or in German, *Geist.* Reason and nothing but "reason" or "idea", the *true,* the *eternal,* and the absolute *powerful essence,* reveals itself in the world in its unfolding manifestations.[131] History, for Hegel, was "the development of the spirit *in time*", while nature was "the development of the idea *in space*".[132] Both were held to be manifestations of the spirit. Both result from the spirit (reason, idea or God, all of which are identical) working itself out in the world and under the conditions of finitude.

Of utmost import for Hegel was the differentiation between the particular and the whole, on the one hand, and between the ideal and the real, on the other, because it was this differentiation which give rise to his dialectical process of *thesis-antithesis-synthesis*. Since only the totality of reality, or wholeness, is true, and reality necessarily presents itself only in particulars, the ideal is necessarily distinct from the real.[133] Being a *part* but not the *whole,* every individual aspect of reality necessarily carries its negation with it. This negation, however, which causes a contradiction within reality itself is not a negative quality as far as the process of the onward moving realization of the spirit is concerned. Rather, the negation is necessary to the realization of the spirit which comes about as the spirit continually unites with itself and diverges from itself in its different manifestations. The uniting and diverging constitute the ebb and flow of the dialectical movement — thesis, antithesis and synthesis — in the process of self-realization. Being invokes non-being which synthesizes in new being in the process of becoming. Reason, God, Spirit, idea, in short, "transcendent reality", is thus realized in world reality through an evolutionary movement from the lower to the higher and from the simple to the complex as the whole moves on its way to inevitable completion. In short, the universe, including thought, humankind, culture, the state, law, ethics, etc., results from mind in the process of self-realization which, in turn, is the realization of all selves and entities of both history and nature in the process of self-creation.[134]

Though there is no belying the magnificence of this most complete and in many ways most profound of metaphysical systems, there is also no denying the price of Hegel's forced monistic scheme. The result is a romantic unification of all reality with a consequent loss of transcendence.[135] God, spirit, and mind are identified with the ongoing dialectical process of history. History itself and indeed the totality of reality are so dependent upon negative as well as positive factors and so ~~revitalized~~ relativized in relationship to an eschatological whole that criteria within the process, even those criteria which might be called for differentiating negative from positive factors, are difficult to come by.

In his attempt to overcome Kant's dualism and individualism, Hegel emphasized a future wholeness where final reality is reached and final answers are given. The individual knows truth only in recognizing it in the other. The individual realizes itself only in relationship to others in the whole. It is only in relationship to family, society, state and eventually history that the individual is given and knows freedom. The result is that just as present freedom and reality are judged in relationship to the purpose of history toward which the whole of reality is moving in dialectical process, so, too, the individual is judged and valued in relationship to that state of existence which can only be defined teleologically.

Art, religion and finally philosophy (for Hegel, the all-inclusive queen of the sciences) are necessarily included in the spirit's drive for manifestation and toward final unity. As the spirit manifests itself in nature via space and in history via time, so it evinces itself in art as visability, in philosophy as thought, and in religion as the relationship to the absolute which is revelation.[136]

Neither space nor time allows for an intensive discussion here of Hegel's integration of philosophy and the faith, but it is a matter of highest importance that we understand that at the very basis of Hegelianism, which is the foundation of Marxist materialism, on the one hand, and idealistic-oriented Protestantism, on the other, there lies a refusal to recognize God as transcendent. Here it is well to be reminded again that Hegel studied theology before moving into philosophy. It can be argued that rather than having left theology, he wrote theology in a philosophical mode. Indeed, for Hegel as for Thomas Aquinas, philosophy and theology were essentially the same thing. Both were manifestations of the spirit.[137]

As Richard Kroner points out, Hegel accused the Reformers of cutting the bond of amity between knowledge and faith, between human, intellectual and divine revelation, between the temporal and the eternal.[138] The effect was to deepen the dualism between the human sciences and the natural sciences.

> In science . . . thought must be subordinate to what is given to the realities of fact . . . while philosophy dwells in the region of self-produced ideas, without reference to actuality.[139]

Hence, rather than helping us out of our Kantian dualistic predicament, Hegel, it would seem, further confused matters. He continued Kant's epistemological dualism between faith and natural science and introduced a dualism of an even more devastating variety of his own — that between the imperfect present and the perfect future. The present is given over to a thesis-antithesis-synthesis process where, as in Schelling, it is only through the dualism of contradictory forces that a living movement is possible.[140] In addition, according to Hegel, it is only in the future, when the state of perfection is reached, that the present can really be judged. Even worse, if it is criteria that matter, since both positive and negative are manifestations of the same spirit, it is difficult if not impossible to choose between them even in retrospect. In fact, they are necessary to one another and pass over into one another:

> The bud disappears when the blossom breaks through, and we might say that the former is refuted by the latter; in the same way when the fruit comes, the blossom may be explained to be the false form of the plant's existence, for the fruit appears as its true nature in the place of the blossom.[141]

Only in the end, then, will knowledge really be possible. Tentativeness and approximation are, of course, of the nature of finitude itself. Hence, even the Apostle Paul could say, "We see as in a glass darkly, but then face to face. Now I know in part, then I shall understand fully" (I Cor. 13:12). However, to base truth on eschatological knowledge alone as Hegel did is to abandon the present and hence to shift our rational facilities into neutral. Thus, in the end, this most rational of systems would seem to imply the abandonment of reason.

If by denying the power of thought to penetrate into the essence of things (*das Ding an sich*) and by dividing faith from science, Kant began a trend in Protestantism which opened it to the danger of subjectivizing and spiritualizing the faith to such a degree that it had little to do with the real world,[142] Hegel's absolute idealism was hardly a correction. There can be little quarrel with his intention to re-establish the unity of reality by attempting to overcome the Cartesian-Kantian dualistic understanding of reality and thus to re-establish a medieval-type synthesis.[143] His idealization of reality and eventual subjectification of it differs little in this regard from the thought of Fichte. Even though, for Hegel, the world was real, it was a world of the mind, of the eternal idea, rather than a world of nature *qua* nature with which he was concerned. Hegel's statement, "The beautiful subjectivity of Protestantism is transformed by the Enlightenment into an empirical subjectivity, and the poetry of its grief . . . into the prose of a satisfaction with this finite world",[144] illustrates this point.

Hegel, of course, was certain that he moved away from Kant

as well as Fichte, both of whom he accused of using their philosophies to investigate man rather than God. "Man and mankind are their absolute principles, namely, a fixed and insurmountable finitude of reason, rather than a reflected splendor of eternal beauty."[145] The way out for Hegel, however, was not to establish any kind of contingency relationship between the sacred and the secular. His solution was rather to resacralize the secular.[146] Hence, in contrast to Kant, for whom religious concepts were but the necessary presuppositions of a moral life, for Hegel, philosophy completed the movement of the Reformation by replacing religion.[147]

In an attempted "advance" on Schelling, who reconciled the absolute ego with nature by making nature itself a part of creative divine power which "pours itself out as material throughout the whole of space",[148] Hegel's *Geist* (mind-spirit) both subsumes the material realm within itself and reconciles itself with human mind. *Geist* is, thus, both human and divine. Absolute mind manifests itself in thinking or idea. Although the idea is not yet complete, not yet a perfect manifestation, to think and to reason is to participate in the divine itself. "God is revealed, there is nothing secret with regard to God anymore." In an ideal way God is "set in me". "He is set in us."[149]

Philosophy, thus, replaced religion simply because God speaks through it. Philosophy speaks in God and hence for God. The rational is the real because God, the supreme Reason, manifests himself in and as human reason. God, humankind, nature, thinking are all reconciled in a grand unity because in all, God himself — the supreme *Geist* — comes into being.

Little wonder, then that because *thinking* is the highest manifestation of the spirit, eventually revelation will give way to knowledge, and religion including the Christian religion which is "the religion of freedom", will dissolve into philosophy.[150] In the end "philosophy and religion coincide". Even now "philosophy is itself in fact an act of divine worship".[151]

Footnotes to Chapter II

1. Jaki, *Physics,* p. 430.
2. Cf. above, pp. 26 ff.
3. John Cobb, *A Christian Natural Theology Based on the Thought of Alfred North Whitehead* (London, 1966), carries the dedication: "To Charles Hartshorne: To whom I owe both my understanding and my love of Whitehead's philosophy".
4. William Paley, *Natural Theology* (London, 1802), p. 12.
5. *Ibid.,* p. 440.
6. *Ibid.*
7. Cf. below, pp. 63 ff.
8. Samuel Taylor Coleridge, *Confessions of an Inquiring Spirit* (London, 1863), introduced idealism into British theology. T. H. Green's influence at Oxford can hardly be overestimated for British and especially English theology, as we can see in the idealistic orientation of Charles Gore (1853–1932), the Lux Mundi School and the "enlightened" Anglo-Catholicism which it spawned in William Temple, for instance. Alfred North Whitehead's process philosophy is more Berkleian than Kantian, perhaps. However, its kinship with the thought of Hegel (who combined Schellingian organismic concepts with Kantian ideas and ended up with a concept of process which manifests the eternal mind, thus overcoming the dichotomy between subjectivity and objectivity) is perhaps more than coincidental. Josiah Royce, who studied in Germany, was America's foremost representative of idealism and shared with Whitehead an interest in science. Royce, it seems, is the original source for the thought of Charles Hartshorne.
9. A. N. Whitehead, *Process and Reality* (Cambridge, 1929), p. 68.
10. Cf. especially A. N. Whitehead, *Science and the Modern World* (Cambridge, 1926) and *Process and Reality.*
11. William Temple, *Nature, Man and God* (London, 1934), pp. ix, 490.
12. *Ibid.,* cf. esp. pp. 246 ff., "The Transcendence of the Immanent".
13. *Ibid.,* p. 265.
14. *Ibid.,* p. 266.
15. *Ibid.*
16. *Ibid.,* p. 269.
17. *Ibid.,* cf. pp. 86, 87, 111 ff., 121, 162, *et al.*
18. *Ibid.,* pp. 258 ff.
19. *Ibid.,* pp. 160 f. Cf. Whitehead, *Process and Reality,* p. 492.
20. Temple, *Nature, Man and God,* p. 259.
21. *Ibid.*
22. *Ibid.,* cf. Whitehead, *Process and Reality,* p. 497.
23. *Ibid.*
24. *Ibid.,* pp. 257 ff.
25. *Ibid.,* p. 270. The overlap with Whitehead's *Process and Reality* would seem to be such that one may speak of dependence.
26. *Ibid.,* italics added.
27. Whitehead, *Process and Reality, passim,* esp. pp. 486-497.
28. *Ibid.,* p. 486.

29. *Ibid.*
30. Whitehead, *Science and the Modern World*, p. 243 and *Process and Reality*, p. 345.
31. Whitehead, *Science and the Modern World*, p. 250.
32. *Ibid.*, p. 249.
33. *Ibid.*
34. *Ibid.*, p. 250.
35. *Ibid.*
36. A. N. Whitehead, *Adventures of Ideas* (Cambridge, 1933), p. 214.
37. Whitehead, *Process and Reality*, p. 485.
38. A. N. Whitehead, *Religion in the Making* (Cambridge, 1926), p. 57; cf. *Process and Reality*, p. 490.
39. Whitehead, *Adventures of Ideas*, p. 212.
40. *Ibid.*, p. 213.
41. *Ibid.*
42. *Ibid.*, p. 214.
43. *Ibid.*
44. *Ibid.*, pp. 214 f.
45. *Ibid.*, p. 216.
46. *Ibid.*
47. *Ibid.*, p. 217.
48. *Ibid.*, p. 218.
49. *Ibid.*, p. 220.
50. Cf. J. S. Bixler, "Whitehead's Philosophy of Religion", *The Philosophy of Alfred North Whitehead*, ed., Paul Arthur Schilpp (New York, 1941), pp. 489 ff.
51. Whitehead, *Religion in the Making*, p. 156.
52. Whitehead, *Process and Reality*, p. 492.
53. Cobb, *Christian Natural Theology*, p. 169. Italics added.
54. *Ibid.*, p. 225.
55. *Ibid.*, p. 190.
56. *Ibid.*
57. Cf. *Ibid.*, ch. V, pp. 176 ff. for Cobb's entire argument.
58. Whitehead, *Process and Reality*, pp. 486 ff. and *Religion in the Making*, pp. 69 f.
59. Cobb, *Christian Natural Theology*, p. 220.
60. *Ibid.*, p. 179. Whitehead, *Process and Reality*, p. 353.
61. Whitehead, *Process and Reality*, p. 9.
62. Cf. below, n. 66.
63. Cf. above, pp. 45 ff.
64. Cobb, *Christian Natural Theology*, p. 143.
65. *Ibid.*, p. 215.
66. Charles Hartshorne, *A Natural Theology for Our Time* (LaSalle, III., 1967), p. 25; cf. also p. 109.
67. *Ibid.*, p. 6.
68. *Ibid.*, p. 82.
69. *Ibid.*, p. 25. Though Hartshorne's own philosophy would seem to have Roycean as well as Jamesian roots, his appreciation of Whitehead is not

incidental. He applauds Whitehead as being "the only twentieth-century philosopher who recalls Plato to any striking degree". *Ibid.*, p. 115.

70. *Ibid.*, p. 36.

71. *Ibid.*, p. 82.

72. *Ibid.*, p. 60.

73. *Ibid.*, p. 113.

74. For a concise discussion of "panentheism" as compared with "pantheism", cf. *Religion in Geschichte und Gegenwart*, III ed., 7 vols. (Tübingen, 1961), V, 36 ff. Interestingly enough the term "pantheism" seems to go back to John Toland, who under the pseudonymn of Janus Junius Eoganesius published a work entitled *Pantheisticon sive formula celebrandae sodalitatis socraticae* (Cosmopoli, M.DCC.XX).

75. Whitehead, *Process and Reality*, p. 486.

76. *Ibid.*, p. 112. It is thus not coincidental that K. C. F. Krause who, as mentioned, gave *pantheism* its name was also convinced that God was known in an *intuitive relationship*.

77. For a discussion of Schleiermacher, cf. below, pp. 83 ff.

78. Cobb, *Christian Natural Theology*, p. 28. Italics added. We shall see how well Whitehead's "experience" concurs with that of science. Cf. below, pp. 57 ff.

79. Hartshorne is quite candid in admitting that his God is "far from being identical with the God of creatures in general, or even with the God of Abraham", *Natural Theology*, p. 132.

80. Weizsäcker, *Die Geschichte der Natur*, p. 87.

81. Howe, *Mensch und Physik*, pp. 105 ff. and Torrance, *Theological Science*, pp. 59 ff.

82. Whitehead, *Principle of Relativity*, p. 59; cf. also pp. 39, 61 ff. 87 f.

83. *Ibid.*, p. 62; cf. pp. 14-39 and 61-68.

84. A. N. Whitehead, *Modes of Thought* (Cambridge, 1938), pp. 173 ff.

85. *Ibid.*, p. 152; cf. pp. 41 ff.

86. *Ibid.*, p. 181.

87. *Ibid.*, pp. 181 ff. Whitehead's valid concern for wanting to incorporate mind in the reality which mind investigates and move away from the Cartesian dichotomy between *subject* and *object* is the epistemological point of Heisenberg's principle of un-certainty.

88. Cf. below, p. 60.

89. As Northrop indicated, Whitehead's adoption of a Minkowskian world-line to define an electron, as "a sensed adjective qualifying all the event particles in a 'historical route'", is hardly legitimate by Whitehead's own concept of immediate awareness. Northrop, "Whitehead's Philosophy of Science", *The Philosophy of Alfred North Whitehead*, pp. 190 f. with reference to Whitehead, *Process and Reality*, p. 32.

90. Northrop, "Whitehead's Philosophy of Science", pp. 199 ff.

91. Whitehead, *Process and Reality*, p. 177.

92. *Ibid.*, p. 381.

93. Northrop, "Whitehead's Philosophy of Science", pp. 194 ff.

94. Hartshorne, *Natural Theology*, p. 93.

95. *Ibid.*

96. *Ibid.,* Italics added.

97. *Ibid.,* p. 94.

98. Instead of resembling Whitehead's cosmos-dependent God, Hartshorne's "cosmic observer" appears much more like H. S. Murdoch's "fundamental observers". By miraculously being able to observe all points in the universe at once, Murdoch's "fundamental observers" allow for the possiblity of simultaneity. H. S. Murdoch, "Recession Velocities Greater Than Light", *Quarterly Journal of the Royal Astronomical Society,* 18 (1977), 242 ff.

99. Northrop, "Whitehead's Philosophy of Science", p. 168. Northrop refers to Whitehead's *Concept of Nature,* pp. 30, 40, and *The Principle of Relativity,* p. 39.

100. *Ibid.,* pp. 204 f.

101. Whitehead, *Process and Reality,* p. 381.

102. *Ibid.,* p. 106.

103. *Ibid.,* p. 31.

104. *Ibid.*

105. *Ibid.,* p. 94. Cf. William James, *Some Problems of Philosophy* (London, 1911), p. 155.

106. *Ibid.,* p. 113. Since for Descartes the body, as differentiated from mind, represented the "extended" world, Whitehead's statement is simply a protraction of Descartes' basic epistemology.

107. Northrop, "Whitehead's Philosophy of Science", p. 204.

108. In spite of his criticism of Whitehead's philosophy of science, Northrop speaks of it as "the most important achievement in the field in our time". He also adds, however, that Whitehead's system "is not the one on which the scientific and philosophical thought of the immediate future will settle". *Ibid.,* p. 207.

109. Immanuel Kant, *Prolegomena to any Future Metaphysics,* trans., John P. Mahaffy and John H. Bernard (London, 1889).

110. David Hume, *An Enquiry Concerning Human Understanding, Great Books of the Western World,* Vol. 35 (Chicago, 1952), p. 462.

111. *Ibid.,* p. 464.

112. *Ibid.,* p. 462.

113. Immanuel Kant, *The Critique of Pure Reason, Great Books of the Western World,* Vol. 42 (Chicago, 1952), p. 6.

114. *Ibid.,* p. 20.

115. For Kant's critique of Locke's doctrine of common sense and his approval of Hume's scepticism as to the empirical basis of our knowledge of cause and effect, cf. *Prolegomena,* pp. 3 ff. Since, as Norman Kemp Smith points out, Kant was somewhat less than proficient in English, it is most likely that he first read of Hume's *Treatise on Human Nature* in which his argument against causality was expressed, in the German translation of James Beattie's *Essay on the Nature and Immutability of Truth,* in 1772, the same year in which Kant realized the problematic character of *a priori* knowledge of *the independently real.* Cf. Norman Kemp Smith, *A Commentary on Kant's Critique of Pure Reason,* Second Edition (London, 1923), p. xxix.

116. Kant, *Prolegomena,* p. 79.

117. *Ibid.*, p. 78.
118. Hume, *Enquiry*, pp. 463 ff.
119. Kant, *Prolegomena*, p. 78. Is Whitehead's similarity here only coincidental?
120. Kant, *Critique of Pure Reason*, p. 33.
121. Kant, *Prolegomena*, p. 77.
122. Kant, *Critique of Pure Reason*, p. 77.
123. *Ibid.*, p. 83.
124. As indicated, Kantian thought entered Britain largely through the influence of T. H. Green (1836–1882). It joined hands with the romanticism of the Anglo-Catholic movement, itself a legacy of Platonism, and was carried forward through Charles Gore and the *Lux Mundi* School. One can detect this idealistic, romantic Kantian subjectivistic trend in the thought of Whitehead and Temple, as well as in Hartshorne.
125. Karl Barth, *Protestant Theology in the Nineteenth Century* (London, 1972), p. 268.
126. The citation is from Barth on Kant's *What is Enlightenment?* in *Protestant Theology*, p. 268. For Barth's cogent appreciation, analysis and critique of Kant, cf. pp. 266 ff. For an understanding of Kant's epistemology in addition to his *Critique of Pure Reason*, see his *Dissertation (De mundi sensibilis atque intelligibilis forma et principiis);* English translation, *Inaugural Dissertation and Early Writings on Space*, trans., J. Handyside (Chicago, 1929). Dietrich Bonhoeffer's *mündiggewordene Welt* (world come of age) though often misinterpreted in the Kantian sense is not an autonomous world founded on subjectivity for which Kant was responsible. Rather, Bonhoeffer's *mündige Welt* is a world which, though freed from the pre-suppositions of religion, is to be understood with reference to Christ and the Gospel. Bonhoeffer, *Letters and Papers*, p. 229.
127. This relation to the systems of Whitehead and Hartshorne discussed above may be more than coincidental.
128. Cf. J. G. Fichte, *The Science of Knowledge* (London, 1889), pp. 63 ff.
129. Cf. F. W. J. Schelling, *Von der Weltseele* (Hamburg, 1809), pp. viii f., xix f., 3 ff., 8, 17, 27, *et al.* For a discussion of Schelling's epistemology, his opposition to Fichte's *Wissenschaftslehre* and movement back to Kant's *Metaphysische Anfangsgründe der Naturwissenschaft* and *Kritik der Urtheilskraft*, cf. John Watson, *Schelling's Transcendental Idealism* (Chicago, 1882), pp. 75 ff.
130. Edward Caird, *Hegel* (Edinburgh, 1891), p. 128.
131. G. W. F. Hegel, *The Philosophy of History, Great Books of the Western World*, Vol. 46 (Chicago, 1952), p. 157.
132. *Ibid.*, p. 186.
133. *Ibid.*, p. 189.
134. Cf. *Ibid.*, pp. 189 f. For Hegel's dependence on Schelling in this regard, compare Schelling's statements, "In der Natur strebt alles continuirlich vorwärts" ("In nature everything continually progresses forward") and "Die positive Kraft erst erweckt die negative" ("The first thing the positive power does is awake the negative"). Schelling, *Von der Weltseele*, pp. 3, 26.

82 THEOLOGY AND SCIENCE IN MUTUAL MODIFICATION

135. Richard Kroner's point in his excellent introduction to Hegel's philosophical development, "The original unity of all things is for him [Hegel] not the object of a mystical and poetical intuition [as is the case with Schelling and the Romantics] but a truth discovered by logic", is well taken. But it must be remembered that Hegel like Schelling presupposed a basic unity in the structure of his logic. Richard Kroner, *G. W. F. Hegel, Early Theological Writings* (Chicago, 1948), p. 15.

136. Hegel, *Philosophy of History*, p. 176.

137. The revival of Hegel in theological thought by Wolfhart Pannenberg is an attempt at re-recognition of Hegel's contribution.

138. Kroner, *Hegel*, p. 37.

139. Hegel, *Philosophy of History*, p. 156.

140. Schelling, *Von der Weltseele*, p. 17.

141. G. W. F. Hegel, *The Phenomenology of Mind*, 2 vols. (London, 1910), I, 2.

142. The trend is continued to Schleiermacher, Herrmann and Harnack, cf. below, pp. 83 ff., 97 ff., 101 ff.

143. Cf. Kroner's statement, "The movement called 'Enlightenment' had the merit of substituting for the medieval synthesis of opposites a rational, humanistic, secular unity by insisting that happiness is the goal of both reason and life". Kroner, *Hegel*, p. 37 referring to Hegel's *Werke*, I, 3.

144. *Ibid.*, p. 38 citing Hegel, *Werke*, I, 10.

145. *Ibid.*, citing Hegel, *Werke*, I, 15.

146. Hence, it is no coincidence that Marx in his turn could secularize Hegel's philosophy of the sacred. By a simple substitution of the "material" for the "idea", Marx's "dialectical materialism" followed the same all-encompassing dialectical logic as Hegel's "dialectical idealism".

147. Cf. Kroner, *Hegel*, pp. 38 f.

148. Schelling, *Von der Weltseele*, p. 4.

149. Friedrich Heer, ed., *Hegel* (Frankfurt/M, 1955), p. 183.

150. *Ibid.*, p. 233; cf. p. 182.

151. G. W. F. Hegel, *Vorlesungen über die Philosophie der Religion, Philosophische Bibliotek*, I, 29 cited by Barth, *Protestant Theology*, p. 409. For Barth's cogent analysis of Hegel, cf. *ibid.*, pp. 384 ff.

Chapter III

The Idealization of Protestantism

It was the combination of Hegel and Kant, with Schelling and Fichte intervening between the two, which provided the foundation for the nineteenth-century idealization and anthropocentricization of the faith. The individual had become the centre of reality. Divinity had penetrated into humanity and nature. There was a reconciliation and integration of faith and culture, especially culture as influenced by seventeenth-century science. Out of these building blocks neo-Protestant theology was constructed.[1] The theological philosophy of the philosophers was to become the philosophical theology of the theologians.[2]

Schleiermacher's Individualistic Subjectivism

Turning now to theology itself, as far as the development of nineteenth-century neo-Protestantism is concerned, if no one represented the Enlightenment as much as Kant, then certainly no one represented the Enlightenment theology as much as Friedrich Daniel Ernst Schleiermacher. It was, in fact, through Schleiermacher, "the church father of the nineteenth-century", that Kant, "the philosopher of Protestantism", entered theology as such.[3] Kant's individualistic habit of mind was spawned in his home atmosphere of a Lutheran *"pro me"* pietistic perspective; Schleiermacher's was nurtured by the inward-looking pietism of the Moravian Brethren with whom he lived and was educated during his secondary school and early student years.[4]

In Schleiermacher, "the genius of the nineteenth-century in the areas of religion, church and theology",[5] pietism, romanticism, Kantianism and Platonism combined. Kantianism, of course, might be considered a rationalization of Plato in the first place. But Plato, whom Schleiermacher both read intensely while a student and later translated into German, had such a direct influence on Schleiermacher that Schleiermacher himself could say, "I look upon the translation of Plato as my destiny *(Bestimmung)*".[6] Schleiermacher's Platonic idealism thus had both a primary and a secondary (Kantian) source.[7]

In addition to being a Kantian and a Platonist, Schleiermacher was also a romantic. His romanticism was an existential affair. He was an active participant in Berlin's early-nineteenth-century romantic movement which, in a Platonic-Spinozan-Schellingian-Hegelian fashion, understood reality as an essential and non-differentiated unity dominated by the infinite Spirit manifesting itself in the differentiations of finitude. Though Schleiermacher never considered himself a student of Hegel and, for a time, when both were professors in Berlin, he competed with Hegel for influence,[8] Schleiermacher's "spirit-centeredness" and "unity-orientation" were Hegelian indeed. Thus competitors or no, Schleiermacher and Hegel, along with their contemporaries, Schelling and Fichte, drank from the same romantic-idealistic fountain which poured the waters of an original unity into the world where it manifested itself in different droplets, streams, torrents or pools, depending upon the exigencies of finitude defined by time and space.

Schleiermacher, however, was no one's captive. As Hermann Süskind (1879–1914) pointed out in his study of Schelling's influence upon Schleiermacher, an excellent case may be made for Schleiermacher's reaction to Schelling at a crucial point.[9] In the first edition of his book *On Religion, Speeches to its Cultured Despisers* (1799), Schleiermacher's religion depended on "the contemplation of the universal" *(die Anschauung des Universums)*. When, however, a year later, Schelling made this "contemplation of the universal" the backbone of his *System des transcendentalen Idealismus (System of Transcendental Idealism, 1800)* interpreting it as "the understanding, appearance or representation of the infinite in the finite",[10] Schleiermacher reacted with horror at the implications of his own thought ānd from 1805 onward began to think of religion as determined by *feeling (das Gefühl)*.[11] Understandably Schleiermacher then turned on both Schelling and Fichte in critique. Schelling represented, for Schleiermacher, an "aristocracy of the intelligence". His esoteric thought had little to do with life. The philosophy of Fichte, of whom Schleiermacher was once a close friend when both were younger members of the early-nineteenth-century group of Berlin romantics, was considered equally impractical. "A simple positive *'Ich'* and a simple negative *'Nicht Ich'* in no sense provide a world."[12]

Though Schleiermacher might reject the romantic systems of Schelling and Fichte and change his epistemological terminology accordingly, he did not reject romanticism as such. This is best illustrated by the fact, as Heinrich Scholz (1884–1956) pointed out, that Schleiermacher's whole discussion of nature is dependent upon the kind of *Weltseele* (world soul) concept of Baruch Spinoza (1632–1677). Thus, whether or not Schleiermacher was amenable to Schelling's explanations of this "Infinite" or "Universal" manifesting itself as reality under the conditions of finitude (adumbrations of Paul Tillich) in a world of organism (and of A. N. Whitehead), it was just this concept which informed Schleiermacher's interpretation of the world.

Schleiermacher's concept of "Nature" as "a living power"[13] agreed very much with the young Schelling's identification of spirit and nature, "nature as the observable spirit" and spirit as "inobservable nature".[14] Equally Schellingesque was Schleiermacher's statement that "God and the world are correlates so that the world is both the total revelation of divine omnipotence and complete manifestation of his characteristics".[15] Schleiermacher sought to avoid pantheism as such, however. Protecting his source he declared that, since neither he nor Spinoza considered God and the world "a synthetic unity",[16] neither he nor Spinoza were to be considered pantheists. Schleiermacher's effort at this point was directed toward protecting God's transcendence. Hence he was quite sincere in stating that no monistic philosophy was compatible with dogmatics.[17]

The difference here between Schleiermacher and Schelling may be compared to that which we have seen between William Temple and A. N.Whitehead. Schleiermacher and Schelling shared epistemological concepts as did Temple and Whitehead (in the end the four are Platonists), but Schleiermacher, like Temple, is too Christian to allow his basic philosophical concepts to lead him outside the faith. Like Temple's Schleiermacher's biblical orientation caused him to reject the kind of monism proposed by Schelling's romantic idealism. The "divided and conditioned" stood in opposition to God, the plainly unconditioned and simple.[18] Yet Schelling is not easily disposed of, so that if Schleiermacher was not *pantheistic* and so did not identify God with the world, at least he gave evidence of subsuming the world into God and thus of being *panentheistic.* Hence he could say: "The world is the mirror image of Godness [which is] the ground of that which in sum composes the world of ideas."[19] Scholz's statement with reference to Schleiermacher's thought on immanence is to the point: "It is not as if God becomes the world, rather it is closer to the other way around, the progressive raising of the world up to God until at last it disappears in God."[20]

It is true, of course, that Kant too desired to move toward an eventual unity of the totality of reality or reality seen teleologically.[21] Kant could even speak of a "point of union" in the super-sensible for all *a priori* faculties "because no other expedient is left to make our Research harmonious with itself".[22] However, whereas for Kant God is a necessary postulate for conscience or morality,[23] for Schleiermacher God was held to make himself known directly in *das Gefühl* (feeling). "The absolute unity that stands over the opposites and develops opposites out of itself" is not "the world-idea" (as in Schelling) but the "Gottesidee" itself.[24] For Schleiermacher as for Spinoza, existence itself is founded in Godness *(Gottheit)* but is not to be identified with it.

In that Schleiermacher stressed the immediacy of feeling as the way we know God, he had no part of Kant's rationalization by which Kant differentiated between the regulative and constructive principles in reference to God. Rather, for Schleiermacher God was known in much the same way Kant knew beauty. Kant appreciated beauty through the faculty of "taste", which was "the faculty" of judging *a priori* the communicability of feelings that are bound up with a given representation "without the aid of concepts".[25] Thus when Schleiermacher compared revelation to "that prototype of a work of art which produces itself in the soul of an artist",[26] he transferred Kant's explanation of aesthetics into theology.

Reference to Kant's discussion of "aesthetic judgement" and "genius" illustrates the point still further. Kant's aesthetic judgement is *"subjective"*, and though it demands "subjective universality", it is not a "judgement of cognition"[27] and has no "empirical ground of proof". It is by the aesthetic judgement that the beauty of a particular is apprehended,[28] and it is this that would seem directly analogous to the "subjectivized objectivity" of Schleiermacher's *Gefühl* by which the revelation of the divine in humankind is given.

Kant's concept of *genius* which he tied in with his discussion of aesthetics is also applicable to Schleiermacher's thought. For Kant *genius* is the talent (or natural gift) which gives "the rule to Art".[29] *Genius* is "a favourite of nature". A person, the genius is one possessed of "aesthetic judgement" to a supreme degree. In him imagination and understanding concur in such a way that the subjective state of mind is both brought about and is communicated to others.[30] Genius is the exemplary originality of the natural gifts of a subject in the *free* employment of his cognitive "faculties" in such a way that the product "is an example" which is not "to be imitated" but to be followed. "His example produces for other good heads a school, i.e., a methodical system of teaching according to rules so far as these can be derived from the peculiarities of the products of his spirit."[31]

Although Kant's discussion of genius was carried out in relationship to art, were one to make a slight mental shift, one could easily mistake the discussion for Schleiermacher's concept of Christ in *The Christian Faith (Glaubenslehre)*. For Schleiermacher "the perfection of Jesus" is to be seen in his spiritual power. With this power Jesus' God-consciousness overcame the opposing activity of his sensual self-consciousness. In him it was displayed in such spotless purity, with such sovereignty and strength, that it is evident that in his self-consciousness there was the actual being and constant presence of God.[32] Thus, he is the eternal, never failing and adequate source of every further development of spiritual and blessed life.[33] In him alone we find the incommensurable appearance of a spiritual power for which there is no way of accounting.[34] Hence, he alone is necessary for, and the only one who is able to bring about, any possible evaluation of the consciousness of salvation in Christendom.[35] He is the only possible form of perfectability.[36]

Nevertheless, if one reads both Kant's description of "genius", which seems to underlie Schleiermacher's Christ-ology and Schleiermacher's evaluation of Christ carefully, one finds that both the person of genius and, by the same token, Schleiermacher's person of Christ, come close to being expendable. For Kant, the *modus aestheticus* (aesthetic manner) of the genius is in no way to be imitated. Nature has but used him to supply "the rule" according to which "the *feeling* of unity in the presentment alone awaits for beautiful art".[37] Genius, then, to repeat, is "exemplary originality of natural gifts" not to be imitated but only to be followed by one "whom it awakens to a feeling of his own originality".[38]

Likewise for Schleiermacher, in principle, Christian piety could arise apart from its historical connection with Christ.[39] However, in virtue of having possessed "God-consciousness from birth", Christ is the archetype of believers (i.e., the genius).[40] As the one who is "destined gradually to quicken the whole human race into higher life", he is "the Redeemer".[41]

As far as faith is concerned, as Heinrich Scholz pointed out, Schleiermacher went much further than Kant. For Kant faith was simply a necessary *a priori* to morality[42] while, for Schleiermacher, it was constitutive of the human being as such. Thus, Schleiermacher insisted that everyone is born with a religious predisposition.[43] It is something inborn, not attained.[44] The consciousness which constitutes the existence and the "feeling of utter dependence" *(Abhängigkeitsgefühl)* belongs to every one without exception.[45] The feeling of dependence is the unique and the supreme endowment of mankind.[46] Hence, for Schleiermacher, to be human is to be religious and since Christianity is the perfection of the religious consciousness,[47] all religious communities are destined to pass over into and, where possible, to merge with Christianity.[48]

As in any basically romantic system of thought, the over-emphasis on *unity* in the transcendent realm is matched by an over-emphasis on the *individual* in the realm of immanence. Hence, it should nor surprise us that, for Schleiermacher as for Kant, it was the self-sufficient individual who is the centre. As Scholz pointed out, "the *principum individui*" was for him "the mystical in the philosophical arena".[49] The constitution of the individual *qua* individual is of such import, in fact, that for Schleiermacher "one's philosophy depends on one's character".[50] It is an individual construction made of general elements.[51] Hence, it is the "mature individual", the individual dependent only upon his own intuition, the *enlightened* individual freed from both dogma and superstition who is both capable of and responsible for defining reality and hence for doing theology. Here the *sapere aude* (have the courage to make use of your own understanding) which, as noted above, Barth designated as "the watchword of the Enlightenment" in relation to Kant, may be applied to Schleiermacher as well.

As according to Kant the individual self combines intuitive apprehensions and aesthetic judgement with conceptions to define reality of the world, so according to Schleiermacher the individual theologian combines his intuitive apprehension of God through the feeling of utter dependence to define "religious reality"[52] and produce dogma. Theology is thus constituted by "pious self-awareness"[53] or a pious "self-consciousness", and it is just this individualistic subjective cognitive faculty which is basic to both ethics and the Church.[54]

Thus, it is the individual's own private "consciousness of God" which is "the criterion of faith".[55] It is through this *pious self-awareness* or "immediate feeling" of "absolute dependence" that "our own being and that of the infinite being of God are one in self-consciousness". And it is this "personal experience" which is the basis of the doctrines of the faith.[56]

Kant's philosophy was an attempt to provide a metaphysic which was relevant to scientific culture, defined on the basis of Newtonian physics. Schleiermacher can be understood only in relation to his concern to make the faith relevant to culture in general. It was a culture which was influenced by natural science, on the one hand, and the Enlightenment, for which Kantian idealism provided much of the basis, on the other.

Schleiermacher's effort is best evidenced in his *Speeches on Religion* which was directed to the "enlightened sceptics" of his day, that is, those who considered that like Kant they had been emancipated from the dogmatic metaphysical rationalism of the past. As Kant, when challenged by Hume's scepticism as to the reliability of data received from outside the self, had turned for assurance from the objective *outside world* to the subjective *inside world,* so Schleiermacher turned to personal experience as the touchstone of religious reality. In both instances the self became the center.

The coin had flipped. Whereas in the past personal experience in the Christian faith was considered valid if it agreed with biblical teachings and church dogma, now biblical teachings and church dogma were considered valid if and insofar as they coincided with personal experience. Doctrines which are necessary to the faith to exclude heresy, a disease brought about by "foreign influences", were regarded as products of feeling.[57] They "are accounts of Christian religious affections set forth in speech"[58] and take shape when feeling "comes to rest in thinking".[59]

Thus doctrines are accepted or rejected, *emphasized* or *left aside,* on the basis of whether or not they satisfy our present need. They are to be judged as to whether they further the development of the evangelical spirit and whether or not the many revelations in the province of philosophy as well as the natural sciences do not necessitate other definitions. If this is the case we need have no scruples in completely abandoning credal expression.[60] In this sense, Karl Barth was essentially right when, in agreement with Scholz, he claimed that in matters of doctrine Schleiermacher was prepared to "erase and alter what in untimely fashion (!) oppress the apparatus of dogma and hamper the living faith in its attempt to walk hand in hand with the onward marching science".[61]

As for scientific presuppositions, Schleiermacher, like Kant, was convinced of the Newtonian deterministic definition of nature and allowed his dogmatic concepts to be formed accordingly. Dogmatics, he claimed, has a system of its own as do the other sciences.[62] Schleiermacher was careful, therefore, not to allow any particular philosophical system to prescribe the content of dogmatics. Though he realized that dogmatic

language is dependent on philosophical thought, he knew also
that not all philosophical thought is appropriate to dogmatics.
Following his formal refusal of any kind of monism or pantheism, he rejected any type of metaphysic which would make no
distinction between God and the world, good and evil, or the
spiritual and the sensual. Such were judged as *ipso facto* not
appropriate.[63]

Fundamentally, and again at a formal level, there was for
Schleiermacher no opposition between theology and natural
science.

> The religious self-consciousness, by means of which we place all
> that affects or influences us in absolute dependence on God,
> *coincides entirely* with the view that all such things are con-
> ditioned and determined by the interdependence of nature.[64]

Thus, "world-consciousness" and "God-consciousness" are
not in opposition but are ultimately harmonious. Were it
possible to attain a totally pious self-consciousness along with a
complete world consciousness, the combination would produce
"a complete world conception".[65] Hence, Schleiermacher
could define "divine preservations" as "the absolute dependence of all events and changes on God", and "natural causa-
tion" as "the complete determination of all events by the
universal nexus". They are, he contended *"one and the same
thing simply from different points of view"*.[66]

It is in this sense that Schleiermacher did not hesitate to
throw out a challenge in the direction of the traditionalist
camp. He warned those whom he felt were stuck in pre-
Enlightenment thought that if they were to have anything to
say to their own time, they would have to "re-educate"
themselves else they would be subject to the "bombardment of
ridicule", be responsible for "the starvation of all science", and
for a possible fall back into "barbarism".[67] Hence he called
upon those responsible for the formulation of Christian dogma
to present faith in such a way that it at no point contradicted
the recognized principles of nature, on the one hand, and
historical investigations, on the other.[68]

Schleiermacher's struggle to express the relationship
between God and nature came to the fore in his discussion of
miracle. For Schleiermacher, God does not by-pass nature. "It
can never be necessary . . . to interpret a fact [in such a way]

that its dependence on God absolutely excludes its being conditioned by nature."[69] Events, therefore, must be understood with a bias toward their natural causes. "We must . . . try, as far as possible, to interpret every event with reference to the independence of nature".[70]

Thus, though Schleiermacher did not outlaw miracle, he treated it with the greatest scepticism. The reason for this was three-fold. First, the event of miracle would mean that God had not ordered the natural system right in the first place. Second, miracle would imply that there is latent in nature a basic opposition or resistance to God in creation which he must deal with by way of "interference" in the natural system. And third, were one to admit that God needed to perform miracles one would tend to acknowledge that God needed constantly to compensate for the effect of free causes upon nature.[71] In this way God would be pitted against free will. In fact, and here we see Schleiermacher's dependence on a Newtonian deterministic world-view, since a miraculous event bears upon the interconnected chain of all finite causes, "every absolute miracle would destroy the whole system of nature".[72] Hence rather than recognize miracle, Schleiermacher proposed to abandon "the absolutely supernatural",[73] at least as far as nature was concerned.

However, Schleiermacher in no sense ascribed to a Laplacian mechanistic universe. Nature is one thing, he held; humankind is another. The world does not consist of "nature mechanism alone". Rather the world must be understood as the "interaction of the nature mechanism and of free agents".[74] Further, both the "nature mechanism" and the "activity of free causes" may be traced back to God; "the one is as completely ordained by God as the other".[75] Recognition of the mechanistic universe as described by Newtonian physics, on the one hand, and his certainty that human beings are "free agents", on the other, put Schleiermacher in a difficult position. In the end he gave up the mechanistic interpretation of reality largely because such a determinism would be directly dependent upon a kind of divine causality which would destroy the consciousness of freedom and this, in turn, would be destructive of the feeling of *absolute dependence* on which his entire system depended. Hence he argued, "let us attribute to ourselves free

causality along with absolute dependence".[76] Absence of freedom obtains where mechanism reigns, "where a thing does not
move itself and moves other things only insofar as it is
moved".[77] Living things, by contrast, have a "diminished freedom".[78]

The gist of the matter is that since human beings *are conscious* of both *absolute causality* in nature and *free will* in
themselves, both mechanism and freedom must be true. After
all, God ordains "free causes" as well as "natural ones".[79] As
he upholds each system in its being, so he upholds "free
causes". It is obvious, therefore, that the mechanistic interpretation of nature and the consciousness of free will stand in open
contradiction to one another, and it is at least to Schleiermacher's credit that he admitted difficulty. Hence he was
quite willing to accept in principle a concept of the universe as
contingent upon God. He acknowledged that the formula,
"God upholds both the mechanistic universe and free causes",
may be open to censure because it "appears to obscure the
essential difficulties in a superficial way rather than actually
solve them".[80] Nevertheless, it was the best he was able to
offer.

Another indication of Schleiermacher's striving for a kind of
romantic unity which would melt obvious opposites into an
eventual whole was his treatment of evil. Evil, for him, was
subjectively and anthropocentrically defined. Primarily evil
was "God-forgetfulness". In Christ, the archetype, evil as
"God-forgetfulness" was overcome.[81] On a personal level, evil
is signified by the "sad moments of life" over against the
"serene moments". It represses rather than advances life. Evil
has no independent existence, however, for it is "rooted in
universal dependence of God".[82] All the same, it is not to be
regarded as "ordained by God".[83] Like the "negative" in
Hegel, evil for Schleiermacher was "an imperfection". He
thought of it as a prod to progress which disappears with the
increasing development of the good and eventually vanishes
into it.[84]

Scholz was no doubt correct when he said: "What
Schleiermacher intended was an apologetic in which Christianity would protect itself through the reverence it would awaken
by its glorious appearance, through the rigorous discipline of its

own development, through the spiritual loftiness in which it discloses itself, through the richness, fullness, power and freedom of its thought which could challenge any idealism."[85] And again: "There is no work which so binds all the questions of a forward moving Christianity with that progressive idealism so securely and reliably encompasses them as Schleiermacher's *Christian Faith*."[86] True enough, but at what price? The price was that of a too easy identity between faith and anthropocentric culture. The cost was not really appreciated until a century later when the world was to pay for the amalgamation between church and society, Christianity and culture, on the battlefields of World War I.

Ritschl's Culture-Christianity

If Schleiermacher introduced Kant into theology, Albrecht Ritschl, whom we must treat in a somewhat summary fashion, represented the Kantian type of theology in its most comprehensive phase. By synthesizing the emphasis upon *obligation* or *duty,* which Kant spelled out in his *Critique of Practical Reason* and named the "categorical imperative", with Schleiermacher's stress on religious feeling and concern for culture, Ritschl combined Christianity and culture into what, for all intents and purposes, was a full blown *Kulturchristentum* (Culture-Christianity).

Ritschl began his studies as a follower of Hegel and initially leaned in the direction of the left wing of the Tübingen school of Hegelianism made famous by such scholars as Christian Baur (1792–1860) and David Friedrich Strauss (1808–1874). He began his own theological structure, however, by setting aside metaphysics in general and especially that of Aristotle and Hegel, because he was convinced that both were too abstract to express the *real relationships* that he "knew to exist" between God and human life.[87] He found a more palatable system by going back to Kant and consequently, instead of presupposing the spiritually dominant principle of Hegelian unity, he adopted Kant's dichotomy between the "theoretical reason" by which the phenomenological world is conceived and "the practical reason" by which value judgements are passed on the actual world. He then combined these Kantian "insights" with Hermann Lotze's (1817–1881) theory that *value* as such is apprehended not through intellect but, as with Schleiermacher, through a "feeling experience".[88]

Ritschl translated Schleiermacher's feeling of "utter dependence" into "a child-like feeling of utter trust".[89] The Christian faith, he claimed, warrants this "trust" because it is *the faith* which is based on "special revelation".[90] Further, it is the particular faith "within which the perfect knowledge of God is possible", and in practical terms it is the faith which demonstrates "the ideal" of human life.[91] As with Schleiermacher, it is Jesus who provided for Ritschl the archetypal image of this "ideal".[92]

Ritschl's scheme was not individualistically oriented, however. He thought of the believer as motivated through "utter trust". In trusting in God the believer was to engage himself in the practical tasks of the *Kingdom of God*. It was *the Kingdom* as far as Ritschl was concerned that was the proper concern of the faith. The Kingdom is a socio-ethical order which arises in this world from "the community of believers and worshippers". The community of believers and worshippers in turn is derived from Jesus Christ".[93] The Kingdom of God is found wherever there is neighbourly love.[94] As such it is "divinely ordained",[95] "decreed before the foundation of the world",[96] humankind's "spiritual and ethical task", and may even be considered "religious adoration".[97] At the same time the Kingdom expresses the world's "final purpose".[98]

The Kingdom, which is, as said, of this world, takes form in society. It is the larger, all-inclusive dimension of reality which encompasses the particular moral communities in which people participate. Each of these forms an integral part of the Kingdom. Marriage, family, work, civic and social life, as well as the relationship the citizen has to his nation, is each, in turn, such a "moral community". Every "community" has dimensions and obligations of its own but in each, according to Ritschl, the believer both "follows Christ" and "serves the common good" by acting "according to the specific principles which govern each institution".[99] Hence, "fidelity to one's vocation" is, in fact, equated with following the example of Christ.[100]

According to Ritschl, then, the Kingdom of God is a sociopolitical magnitude. It is a Kingdom defined by "ethical virtues and actions", which are "regulated by the conduct of *duty*". The ethical virtues and actions are "the products of a *will* directed toward the purpose that is ultimately good".[101] *"Perfection"* itself is the final goal and *"feeling"* its reward. "Perfection" is the "exercise of religious and moral virtues, in the performance of duties of love regulated by our ethical vocation", and this is accompanied by "a feeling of blessedness".[102] Christianity is to be regarded, then, as the religion of the Kingdom, a Kingdom which is both in the world and of the world. It takes form in the expressions of culture itself.

Ritschl's rejection of metaphysics as well as his concept of the Kingdom of moral ends came from Kant.[103] His emphasis upon *the subjective experience of the effects of grace*, the feeling of being as "a child of God" which gives the impulse for "corresponding personal activity",[104] derived from Schleiermacher. His emphasis on Jesus, as "the proto-type *(Urbild)* of humanity",[105] and his conviction that the Holy Spirit, as normative of the justified and reconciled community, the Church[106], came from Schleiermacher as well.

As over against the "scientific view of man" which made of man a simple constituent part of nature, Ritschl, like Schleiermacher, set religious faith on its own particular ground. However, whereas for Schleiermacher the foundation was a rather amorphous "subjective feeling" of total dependence upon God *(das Gefühl),* for Ritschl, the faith which culminates in the building of the Kingdom of God as the divinely ordained highest good of the community was founded specifically "through God's revelation in Christ".[107] Nevertheless, Enlightenment concerns for the perfection of the individual were regarded in true romantic fashion as the proper outcome of faith. Following an Hegelian scheme, Ritschl conceived of faith and life, the Kingdom and the world, as bound together in a non-differentiable whole. "As a member of the Christian community, one is called to the Kingdom of God"[108] which, "as the product of the Christian community",[109] comprises both virtue and duty[110] and is "the final purpose *(Endzweck)* not only of God himself[111] but of the world as well.[112] The formula is valid except when it is read backwards, as inevitably happens, i.e., "one's highest good is the final purpose of God".

Herrmann's Sentimentalism

Johannes Wilhelm Herrmann (the theological teacher *par excellence* of Karl Barth and the teacher of Rudolf Bultmann as well as of John Baillie (1886–1960) of Edinburgh and Edgar Brightman (1884–1953) of Boston University) took up Ritschl's Christo-centrism as the basis on which faith is set on revelation as its own particular ground along with the emphasis that the locus of theology, as well as that of the theologian, is *in the Church*.[113]

However, in making religious faith a matter of "inner experience" grounded on the inner life of Jesus, Herrmann was nearer to both Kant and Schleiermacher than to Ritschl as far as his basic epistemology was concerned. Herrmann's "inner experience" followed Kant's "intuition" and Schleiermacher's "feeling" as the faculty exercised in religious apprehension. Though Herrmann agreed with Ritschl in insisting that religion has its own basis apart from the realm of natural science as such,[114] in contradistinction to Ritschl, he was concerned to consider religion on its own quite apart from both morality and the kind of rationality at work in natural science.[115]

For Herrmann the realm of religion is not even seen by natural science, much less apprehendable in terms of categories appropriate to science.[116] As with Kant and Schleiermacher, God cannot be thought. He is, however, more than the necessary *a priori* for moral experience that he was for Kant, but as with Schleiermacher he can be "experienced". He is "sensed" as a "spiritual possession".[117] Since God cannot be known through the categories of thought, religion becomes based upon individual sentimentality. It is primarily a unity with God, a "participation in the divine life". Thus though religion fosters the moral personality and is "marked in its direction towards the supreme good", it is not subject to moral value judgements and cannot be judged according to categories of morality. Hence in contradistinction to Kant, Herrmann held that religion does not grow out of the ethical will alone.[118] Religion is certainly related to ethics, but it is in no sense justified by it.[119] Rather religion must "guarantee the truth of its own ideas".[120]

Though Herrmann had tremendous respect for Schleiermacher and even went so far as to designate the first four of his

Speeches on Religion the most important writings to appear since the New Testament,[121] Schleiermacher's idea that religion derived from "the unity of self-consciousness" did not appeal to Herrmann at all.[122] In a real sense Herrmann was much more pessimistic than was Schleiermacher. He was quite convinced, for instance, that "fate not God"[123] controlled existence. He was, therefore, not in the least persuaded that Schleiermacher's "feeling of absolute dependence" related to God. Rather, in that the ground of that "dependence" was neither specified nor specifiable within Schleiermacher's theology, Herrmann was of the opinion that any dependence upon feeling in relationship to *the other* was at best ambiguous. The content of consciousness was "at best *a condition* for the possibility of religion".[124] Rather than being a matter of feeling, the experience of religion, for Herrmann, is to be found in "the secret life of the soul".[125] It is based on a "most compelling experience" of "revelation"[126] and expressed as a "language of love which seeks response".[127] In such and experience, that is, while undergoing this kind of revelation, "we know ourselves to be in the grip of a spiritual power which acts on us as the manifestation of pure goodness".[128] The effect is "a joyful revival of our own soul"[129] which is accompanied by a clear consciousness of "our freedom or inward independence".[130] In the society of our fellows, i.e., in the Church, which is the social locus of the religious experience, such a moment causes us to "experience within ourselves the awakening of reverence and trust".[131]

As religious experience, although primarily individual and subjective, has a social dimension in the church, so it has an *ontic* relationship as well. The reception of revelation gives rise to the experience of "a new reality",[132] which comes about when the Christian perceives himself to be in the presence of a "living power" working within the "inner life which is its hidden realm".[133] In such an experience "we know ourselves to be transported into what, compared with the common life of man, is a new existence".[134] It is in relating this "new existence" to present existence that religious sentiment takes on the kind of knowledge that is completed in the moral personality.

Contrary to Ritschl, for whom the Kingdom of God had to

do with ethical activity concerned for the transformation of society and culture (thus, Ritschl could be seen as the progenitor of the American Social Gospel), for Herrmann, the individual who experiences God under the "direct influence" of "the person of Jesus" encompasses the results of that influence in himself. In a quite pietistic way, the individual who undergoes such experiences becomes a moral personality in being emancipated *from the world*.[135] Hence, whereas for Ritschl the center of faith was the participation of the individual believer in the Kingdom, for Herrmann faith was centered in and completed in the self. The individual, in fact, imbibes the divine. "Jesus himself", who is the "pure manifestation" of the "inner life" of God,[136] so introduces himself into the personal life of the believer that the believer is infused with the "personal life" of Jesus.[137]

In sum, "Christian faith is that renewal of the inner life" which people experience in contact with Jesus as he becomes for them the "revelation of God which is the foundation of God's rule in their hearts".[138] The result is nothing less than "newness of life".[139] The Kingdom, therefore, is not of this world as it was for Ritschl. Rather it is the rule of God in one's own inner self. It brings about "inward transformation", the consequence of which is full submission to God so that God rules over our "souls".[140]

Despite Herrmann's formal disagreement with Schleiermacher's designation of religion as "the feeling of utter dependence", Herrmann is as individualistically subjectivistic as Schleiermacher ever was. Herrmann's high regard for Schleiermacher's *Speeches on Religion* mentioned above was corroborated by his judgement that Schleiermacher was "the first to recognize that the subject of theology cannot be doctrines or dogmas. Rather it was *an inner quickening created in mankind through the power of the Person of Jesus*".[141] It is by this power, according to Herrmann, that we both overcome sin and are "transformed".[142]

Consistent with his emphasis upon feeling and experience in contrast to knowledge, Herrmann was certain that the New Testament portrayal of Jesus had nothing to do with doctrine.[143] Thus Herrmann considers that both John Calvin's *Institutes* and Thomas Aquinas' *Summa,* which construe the faith as consisting in matters of doctrine[144] and demand obedience to God as conceived of in terms of the traditions of the Church were quite contrary to the essence of faith. In contradistinction, the way of the Christian religion for Herrmann was *"the unconditional will to truth"* or "submission to the facts *which we ourselves experience"*.[145] Hence as far as his individualistic subjectivism is concerned, actually Herrmann is Schleiermacherian whether he admits it or not.

For all of his individualistic subjectivism Herrmann continued to find a proper place for both "natural theology" and "ethics". Natural theology did not stand on its own as in Thomas Aquinas, however; rather it provided an addendum to personal revelation. In addition to the experiences of the inner life of Jesus or the power of the person of Jesus in our souls or upon us,[146] Herrmann found the world itself to be an "instrument of God's revelation".[147] Rather than building his ethics on natural law, therefore, as one who takes natural theology as being primary would do, Herrmann founded his moral principles in the person of the believer in the encounter with revelation. Thus Jesus himself who becomes the real power in us when he reveals his inner life to us, which power we recognize *as the best thing* our life contains,[148] enables us to live in accordance with the demands of faith.

With his exclusivist emphasis upon the self, it was no coincidence that Herrmann relativized history to the point of making it of little importance. He thereby set a fateful precedent for much of twentieth-century theology for which historical events are important mainly for the ideas they symbolize. Herrmann's sentence, "The basis of faith must be something fixed; the results of historical study are continually changing",[149] typifies Enlightenment-inspired theology which, much as Schelling, continues to look at the different eras of faith as illustrative manifestations of the eternal God manifesting himself under the conditions of finitude.

In following this Enlightenment trend Herrmann could maintain that the "power of the personality of Jesus" was not disfigured by historical investigation.[150] In contrast to an historical orientation whereby the witness of the past becomes normative for the present. Herrmann was convinced that every believer carried with him "the portrait of Jesus" as the "absolute truth".[151] Jesus needs no intermediary. We "become conscious of God's communion with us most distinctly by the fact that the Person of Jesus reveals itself to us through the power of his inner life."[152]

Reiterating again that communion with God depends upon our "experience of the personal life of Jesus as a real force",[153] Herrmann delineated three ways by which this experience comes about. The initial two of these depend more on the history of the faith than Herrmann might want to admit. The first was "by the way in which Jesus' disciples behave to us". The second, which is difficult to distinguish from the first, was the portrayal of Jesus "in the tradition of the New Testament". In the third way, however, we experience Jesus "out of the joy and amazement that such a thing as the personal life really meets us in the world".[154] In the end then, as is to be expected, it is individualistic subjectivity, "a sentiment" which is the controlling factor in Herrmann's theological thought.

It would seem, therefore, that the Ritschlian school moved with Herrmann into a romantic pietism depending upon individual personal experience of the inner life and thus in a real sense away from Ritschl's social concern and back to Schleiermacher. Contrary to Schleiermacher, however, who, for all his subjective pietism had a real concern both for the world and for science, Herrmann's teaching tended to emancipate the Christian from the world and, over against Schleiermacher, his theology served to sever any kind of concern for science as such.

Harnack's Historicism

Adolf von Harnack, "the dean of liberal theology", attempted to undo the damage of Herrmann's individualistic subjectivism and return to a theology based on historical evidence secured by way of "scientific procedures". From my point of view, it is to Harnack's credit and, therefore, to the credit of the *intention* of nineteenth-century neo-Protestant liberalism from Schleiermacher to Ritschl, of which Harnack, so to speak, was the capstone, that he *attempted,* on the one hand, to overcome the rift between faith and science and, on the other, to heal the hiatus between faith and history. The fact that the "science" Harnack had in mind was Newtonian mechanistic science, however, severely curtailed his theological programme. Nonetheless, like Schleiermacher, he was at least aware that scientific thought impinged upon theological thought. Harnack's attempt to show the relevance of theology to culture, a continuation of one side of Schleiermacher's concern,[155] was in Harnack's situation a re-emphasis of Ritschl's desire to unite the Gospel with western cultural achievement and development. This along with his appreciation for an Herrmannian type of personal inwardness of faith, illustrated by his affinity for the romanticism of Goethe, allowed Harnack to gather up nineteenth-century neo-Protestantism and display both its strength (including the strength of appeal) and its deficiency as far as content is concerned.

Harnack's popularity rested on the apparent immediate relevance of his message. "The essence of the Gospel", to use his own but never defined phrase, was, at least formally, not some sort of escape or emancipation from the world. It was not a retreat from responsibility for culture as it was with Herrmann.[156] Rather Harnack's message was an attempt to proclaim eternal life in the midst of time, life lived in the power of God and in relationship to him. In the end, however, with Harnack as with his nineteenth-century "neo-Protestant" predecessors, individualism and even pietistic inwardness won the day.

For Harnack the message of the Gospel goes back to the historical Jesus himself. Jesus proclaimed not escape from life but freedom and responsibility for the higher things of life here and now. Hence, the Gospel has to do with life in the present. It is centered in this world and is the foundation of moral culture. It is no surprise, therefore, to find that Harnack, like Ritschl, paid little or no attention to the New Testament's eschatological dimension of the Kingdom. He rejected specifically the eschatological message of John the Baptist.[157]

Contrary to Ritschl, however, Harnack held that the Christian religion "is no ethical or social *arcanum* for the preservation or improvement of things generally".[158] Rather, as with Herrmann, "The Kingdom" is "the rule of God" in the hearts of individuals.[159] It is "within you".[160] It is where God enters time[161] or, " 'it is in the midst of you' a still and mighty power in the hearts of men".[162] Here we see that in spite of Harnack's attempts to move beyond pietistic inwardness and be relevant to life here and now, life lived responsibly in community, it is doubtful if his epistemological foundations allowed him to carry out his own intention. Harnack's discussion of dogma is a case in point. For him dogma did not have its basis in community. Rather its history is "in the individual living man and nowhere else".[163] Exactly as for Schleiermacher, therefore, dogma for Harnack was the attempt to give expression to individual religious apprehension[164] and in the end it is just this individualism which allowed Harnack both to subvert his profound historical learning to the "needs" of the present and to wrap theology around his social and cultural concerns.

In fairness to Harnack, however, it must be pointed out that he could also insist that dogma was normative. It determines and should determine "religious feeling".[165] More importantly, "Christianity without dogma, that is, without a clear expression of its content, is inconceivable".[166] Harnack's continuation of the Enlightenment tradition of relativizing dogma was both positive and negative. Positively it enabled him to see doctrine in the context of the ongoing life of the Church and hence as subject to development. Negatively, however, it also gave him licence to regard it or disregard it in the light of contemporary culture. This is nicely illustrated by Harnack's statement in which he at one and the same time insisted that dogma was "necessary for the expression of faith", but also claimed that the necessity of dogmatic statements *"does not justify* the unchangeable permanent significance of that dogma which has once been formed under definite historical conditions".[167]

In sum Harnack's effort to reconcile Christianity and culture was an attempt to reassert the synthesis between faith and civilization that the influences of the Enlightenment had tended to dissolve. Methodologically Harnack picked up once more the historical emphasis of the Tübingen school.[168] He adopted thereby an Hegelian concept of progress (though without the Hegelian dialectic) to show the advance of theological thought (dogma) from the beginning of the Judaeo-Christian faith in the Old Testament to its proper manifestation in Lutheran Protestantism. Lutheran Protestantism, he held, was nothing less than the "re-establishment of Pauline Christianity in the spirit of a new time".[169]

Harnack's goal, then, was to show how the *essence* of Christianity or "the Christian religion" (as he significantly preferred to call the Christian faith) works itself out or is manifest in the different eras of the Church. Beginning with apostolic times he traced the development through the era of the Church fathers, where dogma arose as "a work of the Greek spirit on the soil of the gospel",[170] to its culmination as seen in the Protestantism of Luther. It was Luther's thought, Harnack insisted, which opened up the way for the Gospel *not* to be indentified with dogma;[171] and if we remember the *pro me* (for me) emphasis of Luther whereby the emphasis was upon the saving work of Christ as experienced by the individual, Harnack's judgement in this regard may be correct. The Gospel, however, may well have suffered as a result.

For all Harnack's insistence upon the "essence" of the faith, if we ask for a determination of what this "essence", which manifested itself in the different eras of the faith, actually is, we are not given an answer. Surely it is true, as Harnack claimed, that if we are to talk about development we have to identify that which develops. Hence Harnack stated:

> Progress is finally dependent on a true perception of what the Christian religion originally was, for this perception alone enables us to distinguish that which sprang out of the inherent power of Christianity from that which it has assimilated in the course of its history.[172]

We would expect therefore that Harnack would tell us what the faith originally was and what was later "assimilated". However, he does not.

Rudolf Bultmann, who was in no sense negatively critical of Harnack, came to the same conclusion. In his "Introduction" to the recent edition of Harnack's *Wesen des Christentums* Bultmann wrote, "Despite the fact that Harnack undertook the task of describing the essence of Christianity in the spirit of an historian primarily, he nevertheless never portrayed the *essence itself* as an historical phenomenon".[173] "The essence", then, is something beyond history. It is, we may say, "meta-historical".[174] Like Kant's "thing in itself", it is not specified. This "essence" is "something with a history subject to development"[175] rather than being a product of evolution, as Bultmann points out. Hence it takes on different manifestations from time to time.[176] It makes itself evident as it progresses through the different eras of the history of the Church.[177] "Every episode carries us forward and retrogressions are unable to undo that progress."[178]

In the end Harnack at least points to the place where "the essence" may be uncovered. It is to be found in the Gospels and specifically in the pronouncements of Jesus. Hence Harnack could lock arms with Johann Wolfgang Goethe (1749–1832) and quote him with approval:

> Let intellectual and spiritual culture progress, and the human mind expand, as much as it will; beyond the grandeur and the moral elevation of Christianity, as it sparkles and shines in the Gospels, the human mind will not advance.[179]

The Gospels, according to Harnack, are reliable histories. They "offer us a plain picture of Jesus' teaching".[180] There we find Jesus whose "words breathe peace, joy and certainty" living "in continual consciousness of God's presence".[181] Hence, as for Schleiermacher, Christ was totally possessed of "God consciousness",[182] so for Harnack Christ's mind was "wholly concentrated on the inner relation of the soul with God".[183] Significantly Jesus' message was not necessarily new or unique. His teaching which expressed "the whole Gospel" combined the ideas "God, the Father", and "Providence", along with "the position of men as God's children", and "the infinite value of the human soul". Hearing the message raised people to their highest level by reminding them *of what they already knew because it lives in the inmost parts of their souls*.[184]

As with Herrmann, so with Harnack, religion which is primarily a matter of inner subjectivity also has an ethical dimension. Jesus' commandment of love showed that ethics has to do with "intention".[185] Religion, in fact, is "the soul of morality".[186] The Gospel is not ascetic, however. Though there are strictures against "mammon"[187] and "selfishness",[188] the world's blessings are to be treated as gifts of God. "Your heavenly Father knows that you have need of all these things."[189]

Thus the Gospel was part and parcel of the mores of religious *bürgerlich* (pious bourgeois) society of which Harnack was both a member and an exponent. His attitude toward justice and defence which, like the rest of his theology and life-style, is grounded in "Jesus' teaching", illustrates the point. "Jesus, like all truly religious minds, was firmly convinced that in the end God will do justice."[190] Ultimately, therefore, earthly rights are "of little account".[191] Hence "Jesus' disciple is to show love to his enemies and disarm them by gentleness".[192] Harnack was also convinced, however, that since Jesus had "the individual in mind, and the abiding disposition of the heart in love",[193] he had no intention of renouncing "the pursuit of our rights in the face of enemies". "Are we to use no weapons but those of gentleness? Are nations not to fight for house and home when they are wantonly attacked?", Harnack asked.[194] The answer was obviously, "No". Hence though the words, "My kingdom is not of this world . . . forbid all direct and formal interference of religion in worldly affairs",[195] Harnack claimed that they do not prevent the Christian citizen from coming to his country's cause. Some fourteen years after writing these words, pious bourgeois Harnack, true to character and to his understanding of the Gospel, would compose the Kaiser's "Declaration of War".

Harnack's ability to bend the Gospel to his will, making accommodations where necessary, is also obvious in his juxtaposition of his understanding of nature, on the one hand, and of prayer, on the other. As to nature, Harnack accepted the Newtonian-Laplacian world view that "the order of Nature" is "inviolable".[196] Miracles interpreted as interruptions in nature "do not happen" and he explained away the New Testament accounts of them.[197] And yet like Schleiermacher Harnack was not quite certain. "We are not yet by any means acquainted with all the forces [of nature]."[198] "In the realm of the influence of soul on soul and soul on body", he asked, "who can still maintain that any extra-ordinary phenomenon that may appear in this domain is entirely based on error and delusion?"[199] Thus over against his "scientific understanding" of nature, and again like Schleiermacher, Harnack is quite convinced that as persons we are not "helplessly yoked to inexorable necessity".[200] In the end God himself is the basis of freedom. For God not only exists, he rules and governs. Further we can influence this ruling and governing, this power over nature by prayer and make that power part of our experience.[201]

Thus for Harnack the Gospel had implications which were unreservedly practical. Nevertheless, in the final analysis Harnack, like Herrmann, held that the Gospel was not of this world. Religion had to do with "God and the soul, the soul and its God".[202] Essentially it required emancipation from this world, a concentration on a higher realm. Hence Harnack criticised "the Pietists" who made Jesus serve as an example for their various callings.[203] He reverted back to the Hellenistic ideal which took leisure to be a delight and labour a drudgery. "Head, hands and feet rejoice, the work is done."[204] Not even "the progress of civilization", welcome as it was, could represent the ideal.[205] The ideal was rather that romantic something beyond and above this life. It was that object of longing romantically intuited and expressed by Goethe:

> *Man sehnt sich nach des Lebens Bächen*
> *Ach! nach des Lebens Quelle hin.*[206]

which, transferred with some poetic licence into English, might read:

> One yearns for life's living streams
> Oh! to go to the very source of life itself.

The romantic appeal, the otherworldliness, the sophisticated piety which essentially escapes life rather than engages it at its roots, is amply illustrated in a paragraph:

> Gentlemen, when a man grows older and sees more deeply into life, he does not find, if he possess any inner world at all, that he is advanced by the external march of things, by "the progress of civilization". Nay, he feels himself, rather, where he was before, and forced to seek the sources of strength which his forefathers also sought. He is forced to *make himself* a native of the kingdom of God, the kingdom of the Eternal, the kingdom of Love: and he comes to understand that it was only of this kingdom that Jesus Christ desired to speak and to testify, and he is grateful to him for it.[207]

The Gospel, then, is to be regarded as timeless. It is based on "the antithesis between the Spirit and flesh, God and the world, good and evil".[208]

In true idealistic fashion "there is a unity underlying this opposition"[209] but the unity can be attained only "by struggle" and then only "approximately". "It is by self-conquest that man is freed from the tyranny of matter." Goethe again expressed the truth for Harnack in this regard.

> *Von der Gewalt die alle Wesen bindet*
> *Befreit der Mensch sich der sich überwindet.*[210]

which we may perhaps render:

> From the power which all creation binds
> He who overcomes himself, himself freed finds.

This Gospel, according to Harnack, marked the end of an era. It was the Gospel according to the Enlightenment. It was anthropologically centered, feeling oriented and romantically inclined. It could consider itself scientific only because, following Kant, it could essentially divide natural science and the "scientific" procedures it used to investigate the history of faith from the way it came to "know" the "essence" of faith. Essentially, however, except in the case of Ritschl where faith was dissolved into culture and vice versa, faith remained *Weltfremd,* foreign to the world. In a strange way and yet in a way that is not so strange, faith accommodated itself to the world or at least to that world of which its representatives were a part. It became a culture Christianity, a *Kulturchristentum,* simply because it was primarily the individualistic personally-oriented religion of the bourgeoisie, those who made culture what it was. And, as the bourgeoisie had little difficulty in adapting themselves to the culture which they had created and which, in turn, created them, so theology and culture marched hand in hand largely oblivious of "the real world" because the hearts and minds of its creators were oriented in a "higher" world. This "higher world" for the most part, however, was little more than the idealized projection of the "good life" the bourgeoisie already enjoyed. It was, to take a cue from William James' well-known phrase with reference to God, that "everlasting more" co-terminus with the best that everyone was able to achieve for himself or herself.

Real transcendence and, hence, radical critique either of this world or of faith was gone. Religion only reminded people "of what they already knew because it lived in the innermost parts of their souls", as Harnack put it.[211] Religion raised humankind to a higher level but it did not demand radical change, nor could it. It had become basic to human identity and basically humanity was in good order. Everything was "OK", to employ an overused American cliché. A little improvement was demanded here and there. Faithfulness could be improved, moral standards more strictly observed, and generosity enhanced so that people might be inspired to love and care for one another but nothing radical could be entertained, for to be radical would mean a break with the *status quo* and the *status quo* was good.

Radicality was to come. It was to come, however, only after the shock of "The Great War". World War I showed just how un-Christian this "Christian culture" was, how ineffective this pious religiosity which gripped the heart but not the world could become. Unbelievably or perhaps not unbelievable at all considering the grip culture had on "faith", when war came the majority of the German Enlightenment-oriented neo-Protestant theologians immediately and enthusiastically closed ranks behind the Kaiser and the admired and even revered Adolf von Harnack led the procession.

Footnotes to Chapter III

1. This in spite of the fact that Kant himself is quite clear in declining to make of nature an "intelligent being" or to place an intelligent being above it "as its Architect". Immanuel Kant, *Critique of Judgement*, trans., J. H. Bernard (London, 1914), p. 290.

2. For Kant's theology, cf. *ibid.*, pp. 61, 259 ff.

3. Kant is so named by J. Kaftan, Schleiermacher by C. Lülmann. Cf. C. Lülmann, *Schleiermacher der Kirchenvater des 19. Jahrhunderts* (Tübingen, 1907); Werner Schultz, *Kant als Philosoph des Protestantismus* (Hamburg, 1961); Cf. Barth, *Protestant Theology*, pp. 425 ff. and Karl Barth, *Die Theologie Schleiermachers 1923/24*, ed. Dietrich Ritschl (Zürich, 1978).

4. Schleiermacher was schooled by the *Brüdergemeinde* from the age of fourteen in Niesky and was later a student in the *Herrenhuter* Seminary in Barby. It is well to remember, as T. F. Torrance has pointed out, that Luther's original emphasis on *pro me* was asserted in relation to the freeing of the self from the self and easily becomes distorted into, not what Christ *has done for me*, but what *he means for me*, as is the case in the theology of Rudolf Bultmann. Torrance, *God and Rationality*, pp. 58 ff.

5. Lülmann, *Schleiermacher*, p. 1.

6. Freidrich Schleiermacher, "Brief an Alexander Dohne", *Briefe an die Grafen zu Dohna* (Berlin, 1887), No. 29 cited by Heinrich Scholz, *Christentum und Wissenschaft in Schleiermachers Glaubenslehre*, Zweite Ausgabe (Leipzig, 1911), p. 20, n. 2.

7. Stephen Sykes' designation of Schleiermacher as "a Platonist" is thus legitimate though he is not only a Platonist. Stephen Sykes, *Friedrich Schleiermacher* (London, 1971), p. 50. Evidence of Platonic influence on Kant may be found in his *Critique of Judgement*, pp. 263 f.

8. Barth, *Protestant Theology*, pp. 426 ff.

9. Herrmann Süskind, *Der Einfluss Schellings auf die Entwicklung von Schleiermachers System* (Tübingen, 1909), pp. 69 ff.

10.. *Ibid.*, p. 154.

11. *Ibid.*, p. 139. Cf. Scholz, *Christentum*, p. 18.

12. Friedrich Schleiermacher, *Dialektik* (Berlin, 1839), par. 196, 2 cited by Scholz, *Christentum*, p. 34.

13. Friedrich Schleiermacher, *Der christliche Glaube*, Zweite Ausgabe, 2 vols. (Berlin, 1830-31), I, 185.

14. F. W. J. Schelling, *Ideen zu einer Philosophie der Natur* (Leipzig, 1797), p. 56. Schelling's *Von der Weltseele* is a continuation and refinement of his argument that reality is the spirit's realization of itself. Cf. above, Ch. II, fn. 129.

15. Schleiermacher, *Christliche Glaube*, I, 242.

16. *Ibid.*, p. 277.

17. *Ibid.*, p. 166.

18. *Ibid.*, II, 340.

19. Friedrich Schleiermacher, *Dialektik* (Berlin, 1831), p. 526 cited by Scholz, *Christentum*, p. 169.

20. Scholz, *Christentum*, p. 170. Scholz calls Schleiermacher's "Pantheism", "'*Akosmismus*' which is close to the Apostle Paul's thought".
21. Immanuel Kant, *Critique of Teleological Judgement*, trans. James C. Meredith (Oxford, 1928), esp. pp. 75-149.
22. Kant, *Critique of Judgement*, p. 235.
23. Cf. Immanuel Kant, *Religion Within the Limits of Reason Alone* (Chicago, 1934), pp. 45, 131 ff. and *Critique of Judgement*, pp. 278 ff. 305 and especially 374 ff. Note that Kant does not infer God from design or argue for his existence on the basis of theology.
24. Schleiermacher, *Dialektik* (1839), par. 134. 1,2,3 cited by Scholz, *Christentum*, p. 40.
25. Kant, *Critique of Judgement*, p. 173.
26. Schleiermacher, *Christliche Glaube*, I, 99.
27. Kant, *Critique of Judgement*, p. 152.
28. *Ibid.*, pp. 150 ff.
29. *Ibid.*, p. 188.
30. *Ibid.*, pp. 201 f.
31. *Ibid.*, p. 204.
32. Schleiermacher, *Christliche Glaube*, II, 61.
33. *Ibid.*, p. 33.
34. *Ibid.*, p. 98.
35. *Ibid.*, I, 71.
36. *Ibid.*, II, 34.
37. Kant, *Critique of Judgement*, p. 205. The *modus aestheticus* thus stands in contradistinction to the *modus logicus*.
38. *Ibid.*, pp. 203 f.
39. Friedrich Schleiermacher, *The Christian Faith*, English translation of the Second German Edition (Edinburgh, 1928), p. 44.
40. *Ibid.*, p. 57.
41. *Ibid.*, pp. 63 f.
42. Scholz, *Christentum*, pp. 175 ff.
43. Friedrich Schleiermacher, *Über die Religion, Reden an die Gebildeten unter ihren Verächtern* (Göttingen, 1899), p. 144.
44. Schleiermacher, *Christliche Glaube*, I, 30.
45. *Ibid.*, p. 244.
46. *Ibid.*, II, 561.
47. Friedrich Schleiermacher, *Christliche Sitte* (Berlin, 1843), p. 27 cited by Scholz, *Christentum*, p. 187.
48. Schleiermacher, *Christliche Glaube*, II, 270, 312.
49. Scholz, *Christentum*, p. 38.
50. Friedrich Schleiermacher, *Briefe*, IV (Berlin, 1863), No. 575 cited by Scholz, *Christentum*, p. 38.
51. Friedrich Schleiermacher, *Ethik* (Berlin, 1835), p. 363 cited by Scholz, *Christentum*, p. 38.
52. Schleiermacher, *Christian Faith*, pp. 12 ff.
53. Barth, *Protestant Theology*, p. 454.
54. Schleiermacher, *Christian Faith*, pp. 5 ff.
55. *Ibid.*, p. 17.

56. *Ibid.*, pp. 131 ff. Note the similarity to Whitehead's "immediacy". Also Tillich's dependence on Schleiermacher's "absolute dependence" is obvious here.

57. *Ibid.*, p. 95.

58. *Ibid.*, p. 76.

59. *Ibid.*, p. 10.

60. *Ibid.*, p. 145.

61. Scholz, *Christentum*, p. 122 cited by Barth, *Protestant Theology*, p. 446.

62. Schleiermacher, *Christian Faith*, p. 122.

63. *Ibid.*, pp. 118 f.

64. *Ibid.*, p. 170. Italics added.

65. *Ibid.*, pp. 173 f.

66. *Ibid.*, p. 174. Italics added.

67. Cf. Friedrich Schleiermacher, *Sendschreiben*, No. 614 cited by Scholz, *Christentum*, p. 124.

68. Schleiermacher, *Christliche Glaube*, I, 210.

69. Schleiermacher, *Christian Faith*, p. 178.

70. *Ibid.*, p. 179.

71. *Ibid.*

72. *Ibid.*, p. 181.

73. *Ibid.*, p. 183.

74. *Ibid.*, p. 180.

75. *Ibid.*, p. 189.

76. *Ibid.*, p. 191.

77. *Ibid.*

78. *Ibid.*

79. *Ibid.*, p. 192.

80. *Ibid.*

81. *Ibid.*, p. 54.

82. *Ibid.*, p. 185.

83. *Ibid.*, p. 187.

84. *Ibid.*

85. Scholz, *Christentum*, p. 122.

86. *Ibid.*, p. 201.

87. Albrecht Ritschl, *Theologie und Metaphysik* (Bonn, 1881), pp. 8 ff.

88. Cf. Philip Hefner, "Albrecht Ritschl, an Introduction", *Three Essays*, pp. 27 ff., for an insightful account of Ritschl's dependence on his Göttingen colleague, Hermann Lotze.

89. Albrecht Ritschl, *Unterricht in der christliche Religion* (Bonn, 1875), par. 46, p. 38. Cf. Barth, *Protestant Theology*, p. 657.

90. Ritschl, *Unterricht*, pars. 1, 2, p. 1.

91. *Ibid.*, par. 55, p. 46. Cf. Barth, *Protestant Theology*, p. 660.

92. Ritschl, *Unterricht*, par. 22, pp. 19 f. Cf. Barth, *Protestant Theology*, p. 660.

93. Ritschl, *Unterricht*, par. 5, p. 3.

94. *Ibid.*, pars. 5 f., pp. 3 f. Cf. Barth, *Protestant Theology*, p. 658.

95. Ritschl, *Unterricht*, par. 5, p. 3.

96. *Ibid.*, par. 14, p. 11.
97. *Ibid.*, par. 4, p. 2.
98. *Ibid.*, par. 14, p. 11.
99. *Ibid.*, par. 8, p. 6.
100. *Ibid.*, par. 9, p. 7.
101. *Ibid.*, par. 63, p. 55. Cf. Barth, *Protestant Theology,* p. 655, where Barth points out that Ritschl's theology is centered on the practical living of the Christian life which at one and the same time answered to the demand of nineteenth-century science that man conceives the world and lives in it "in the best sense according to reason".
102. Ritschl, *Unterricht,* par. 76, p. 67. Italics added.
103. Barth, *Protestant Theology,* p. 655.
104. Ritschl, *Unterricht,* par. 46, pp. 38 f.
105. *Ibid.*, par. 22, p. 19; par. 55, p. 51.
106. *Ibid.*, pars. 22, 55, 59, 86, pp. 19-79.
107. *Ibid.*, par. 5, p. 3.
108. *Ibid.*, par. 55, p. 46.
109. *Ibid.*, par. 5c, p. 3; par. 35, p. 29.
110. *Ibid.*, pars. 63-75, pp. 55-67.
111. *Ibid.*, pars. 13, 23, 24, 43, 45, 46, 57, pp. 11-49.
112. *Ibid.*, pars. 12, 14, 28, 36, 72, pp. 9-63.
113. Eberhard Busch, *Karl Barth's Lebenslauf* (München, 1975), p. 6. As indicated above, Ritschl also influenced Bultmann as well as Tillich by way of Martin Heidegger whose philosophy "can be construed as a direct elaboration of Ritschl's methodological decision to avoid meta-physics by turning to the self-consciousness". Hefner, "Introduction", *Three Essays,* p. 42. It should not be overlooked, however, that Heidegger himself wrote his *Sein und Zeit (Being and Time)* in conscious relation to Wilhelm Dilthey who himself was influenced by Schleiermacher's emphasis on *Innerlichkeit.* Martin Heidegger, *Being and Time* (New York, 1962), p. 429; cf. also pp. 449-455, *et al.*
114. Wilhelm Herrmann, *Systematic Theology* (New York, 1927), p. 21.
115. Cf. *ibid.*, especially pp. 25 ff. Hence, Barth learned from Herrmann that theology itself could have its own scientific seriousness. Busch, *Karl Barth,* p. 56.
116. Herrmann, *Systematic Theology,* p. 17.
117. *Ibid.*
118. *Ibid.*, p. 27.
119. *Ibid.*, pp. 34 f.
120. *Ibid.*, p. 25.
121. Busch, *Karl Barth,* p. 56.
122. Herrmann *op.cit.*, p. 28. The rather rationalistic procedure of "deducing" religion from self-consciousness represents, it would seem, a misunderstanding of Schleiermacher's concept of *Gefühl,* as the human faculty through which God-consciousness arises in the individual.
123. *Ibid.*, p. 29.
124. *Ibid.*, p. 28. Italics added.

125. *Ibid.*, p. 32.
126. *Ibid.*, p. 35.
127. *Ibid.*, p. 33.
128. *Ibid.*, p. 35.
129. *Ibid.*, p. 36.
130. *Ibid.*, p. 35.
131. *Ibid.*, p. 36.
132. *Ibid.*, p. 37.
133. *Ibid.*
134. *Ibid.*
135. *Ibid.*, p. 69.
136. *Ibid.*, p. 51.
137. *Ibid.*, p. 59.
138. *Ibid.*, p. 62.
139. *Ibid.*, p. 63.
140. *Ibid.*, pp. 46 ff.
141. *Ibid.*, p. 64. Italics added.
142. *Ibid.*, p. 65.
143. *Ibid.*, pp. 52 f.
144. *Ibid.*, p. 70.
145. *Ibid.*, p. 152. Italics added.
146. *Ibid.*, pp. 142 f.
147. *Ibid.*, p. 82.
148. Wilhelm Herrmann, *The Communion of the Christian with God* (London, 1906), p. 76.
149. *Ibid.*
150. *Ibid.*
151. *Ibid.*, p. 77.
152. *Ibid.*, p. 79.
153. *Ibid.*, p. 78.
154. *Ibid.* Later when Barth recognized the cultural dependence and extreme individualistic subjectivity of the piety on which Herrmann's thought was based, he, of course, repudiated much of it. However, Barth's continued concentration on Christocentricity and his conviction that faith has its own scientific base apart from natural science, which results in a separation in Barth's thought of theological science from natural science, would seem to have Herrmann, who in these instances depends on Kant and Schleiermacher, as their source.
155. Cf. Schleiermacher, *Reden.*
156. Adolf von Harnack, *What is Christianity?* (New York, 1957). *Das Wesen des Christentums,* initially a powerful and extremely popular series of lectures delivered in Berlin for the general public in the winter of 1899-1900, was printed in book form in 1900.
157. *Ibid.*, pp. 38 ff. Cf. Albert Schweitzer's critique of Harnack in this regard. Albert Schweitzer, *The Quest of the Historical Jesus* (London, 1926), pp. 251 f.
158. Harnack, *What is Christianity?* p. 8.
159. *Ibid.*, p. 56.

160. *Ibid.,* p. 61.
161. *Ibid.,* p. 62.
162. *Ibid.,* p. 54.
163. Adolf von Harnack, *History of Dogma,* 7 vols. (London, 1897), I, 12.
164. *Ibid.,* p. 22.
165. *Ibid.*
166. *Ibid.*
167. *Ibid.,* pp. 22 f.
168. Cf. above, p. 94.
169. Adolf von Harnack, *Lehrbuch der Dogmengeschichte,* 3 vols. (reprinted unchanged from the Fourth Edition, Tübingen, 1909: Darmstadt, 1964), III, 809.
170. Harnack, *History of Dogma,* I, 17.
171. *Ibid.,* p. 20.
172. *Ibid.,* pp. 39 f.
173. Harnack, *What is Christianity?* p. xiii.
174. *Ibid.*
175. *Ibid.*
176. *Ibid.,* pp. 10 ff.
177. Cf. Harnack, *Lehrbuch,* III, 860 where Harnack subjectivizes theology by speaking of it with reference to Luther as *das Bekenntnis des Glaubens zu seinem eigenen Erlebnisse, d. h. zur Offenbarung* (the confession of faith in accordance with its own experience, that is, according to revelation). Cf. also *ibid.,* n. 2. This position, though perhaps having some validity in Luther's struggle against the rationalistic metaphysical theology of the Middle Ages, becomes historicized and individualised in the Enlightenment categories of Harnack's exposition. A continuation of the position can be seen in the existentialistically influenced Lutheran theologians Bultmann and Tillich who subjectivize theology by using Heidegger's existential philosophy to define their anthropology and then shape theology according to the experience of the believer thus defined.
178. Harnack, *History of Dogma,* I, 21.
179. Harnack, *What is Christianity?* p. 4.
180. *Ibid.,* pp. 19 ff.
181. *Ibid.,* p. 38.
182. Cf. above, pp. 81 ff.
183. Harnack, *What is Christianity?* p, 64.
184. *Ibid.,* p. 68. Italics added.
185. *Ibid.,* p. 71.
186. *Ibid.,* p. 73.
187. *Ibid.,* pp. 84 f.
188. *Ibid.,* p. 87.
189. *Ibid.*
190. *Ibid.,* p. 109.
191. *Ibid.,* p. 110.
192. *Ibid.,* pp. 110 f.
193. *Ibid.,* p. 111.

194. *Ibid.*
195. *Ibid.*, p. 115.
196. *Ibid.*, p. 27.
197. *Ibid.*, pp. 28 f.
198. *Ibid.*, p. 27.
199. *Ibid.*
200. *Ibid.*, p. 30.
201. *Ibid.*
202. *Ibid.*, p. 142.
203. *Ibid.*, pp. 117 f.
204. *Ibid.*, p. 120.
205. *Ibid.*, p. 121.
206. Goethe, quoted by Harnack, *ibid.*, p. 121.
207. *Ibid.*
208. *Ibid.*, p. 150.
209. *Ibid.*
210. Goethe, quoted by Harnack, *ibid.*
211. *Ibid.*, p. 68.

Chapter IV

Karl Barth's Break with Enlightenment Theology

The radical break with Enlightenment theology, theology based on individualism and self-consciousness, came with Karl Barth. Barth, who claimed theology to be a science in its own right and pursued it as such, more than any other had seen the basic fallacy of the "natural theology" of both the Newtonian and neo-Protestant kind. Also more than any other he was responsible for the revival of a theology of substance in our time. Nevertheless Barth, like Herrmann, his teacher, was not in a position to consider modern science important to his immediate theological programme. For all his contribution he was never able entirely to overcome the bifurcation between theology and natural science.

Barth's Background

As T. F. Torrance (1913–   ) has pointed out in his trenchant investigation into Barth's early theology:

> Karl Barth's [early] theology falls within the thought-forms of Neo-Protestantism, as represented above all by the great Schleiermacher — that is, the liberal theology of the religious individualism formulated under the impact of the Romantic Idealist philosophy of the nineteenth-century and coordinated with the brilliant culture which it built up.[1]

Barth was "a liberal theologian, even an enthusiastic one, in his youth".[2] His teachers, especially Adolf von Harnack, Hermann Gunkel (1862–1932) and Wilhelm Herrmann, not only repre-

Even so, as Barth pointed out in his interpretation of
the eighteenth century distortions of theology, so in
the nineteenth

118   THEOLOGY AND SCIENCE IN MUTUAL MODIFICATION

sented liberal theology but were its primary voices.[3] From them
Barth learned to swim in the wake of Schleiermacher, for
whom western culture was the very manifestation of Christianity. Ritschl designated its moral purpose, Herrmann gave it
personal   substance   through   individual   internalization
(Innerlichkeit) and Harnack explained its historical development. The result was that Christianity was regarded as culture
and culture as Christianity.

absurd". [12] "Christianity means nothing else than Christ and the
faith of his followers in him; it is something above time, during
century too the Bible was still read in Church even though it
was culturally interpreted.[4] Thus, in spite of the neglect of its
central message, Scripture remained at least the formal basis of
authority for theology in general and for proclamation in
particular. In Barth's particular case, it was the return to
Scripture which he studied in preparation for his weekly task of
proclaiming the Gospel, and especially Paul's *Letter to the
Romans,* that made him aware of a different world, "the
strange world of the Bible". As the world of the Bible moved
into Barth's awareness, he began to sense the deep deficiencies
of his theological education and the theological stance which he
had inherited. He began to see the individualism which separated people from the world and the pietistic leanings of
Schleiermacher mediated through Herrmann as contrary to the
corporateness of the biblical message.[5] Ritschl's emphasis on
the Kingdom here and now, as the end effect of the faith
achieved through duty, did not square with the Apostle Paul's
emphasis on the eschatological character of the Kingdom.
Harnack's developmental optimism with its constant norm of
improvement was incompatible with and stood in direct opposition to New Testament anthropology wherein even "saved
man" remains plagued with sin and its destructive consequences. "For I do not do what I want, but I do the very thing I
hate" (Rom. 7:15).

    And then World War I broke out. It came not only as a
shock which belied the optimistic theory of continual evolutionary progress of "enlightened" nineteenth-century liberalism,
but, for Barth in particular, it came with the agony of the
noisome news that most of his revered theological mentors
stood solidly behind the German war effort. Not only, as

mentioned above, was his once respected teacher, Adolf von Harnack, responsible for drawing up the Kaiser's "Declaration of War",[6] but as if to make matters explicit, the day the war was declared nearly all Barth's theological teachers were among the ninety-three German intellectuals who issued a manifesto which underwrote the Kaiser's military initiative. With that Barth realised how religion and scholarship could be completely transformed into "intellectual 42 cm. cannons". "For me", he wrote, "it was almost worse than the violation of Belgium neutrality".[7]

Now Barth turned away from his idealistic, romantically oriented teachers of nineteenth-century Protestant liberalism who had made the fatal mistake of identifying faith and culture, time and eternity, this world and the next, and ultimately God and human inner consciousness. Barth's ear atuned itself instead to the voices of the critics of both Christianity and culture — Franz Overbeck (1837–1905), friend of Nietzsche and professor for New Testament and Ancient Church History in Basel; the Danish theologian Søren Kierkegaard (1813–1855); and the Russian novelist Feodor Michailovich Dostoevski (1821–1881).

Overbeck's "No" to Culture

Franz Overbeck's *Christentum und Kultur,* published post-humously in 1919, stood in sharp contrast to Harnack's "upbeat" optimistic *Wesen des Christentums* delivered as lectures at the turn of the century.[8] In a lecture entitled *Unerledigte Fragen an die heutige Theologie* ("Unanswered Questions Directed to Today's Theology") Barth was quick to emphasize Overbeck's anti-cultural concept of the faith over against the Culture Christianity which had dominated both theology and Church in the nineteenth and early twentieth-centuries and which had also dominated him as a student.[9] In direct contrast to the amalgam of Christianity and culture offered by Schleiermacher, Ritschl and Harnack, Overbeck found that the Church of the New Testament stood over against culture. The Gospel's concentration on the Kingdom of God and eschatology, "the last things", stood in judgement over and relativized world and history.[10] This world is not eternal but is subject to death. Thus "death" is as effective in witnessing as in destroying".[11] By the same token, "historical Christianity, that is Christianity subjugated to time, is absurd".[12] "Christianity means nothing else than Christ and the faith of his followers in him; it is something above time, during the life-time of Jesus it wasn't even there."[13] As soon as Christianity forgot its immediate relationship to the "last things" and was no longer absolutely critical of things of history, as happened already even in the time of the Apostle Paul, "the history of decay" began.[14] Then Christianity became "a Religion". Religion originates out of the world and shares its origin with the world.[15] "Christianity, however, has no desire to be a religion."[16]

"Historical Christianity",[17] Barth now claimed, is thus a betrayal of the faith and this betrayal which began already with the acculturation of Christianity in the immediate post-New Testament times finally resulted in the nineteenth-century accommodation of Christianity to culture. This "Protestant Jesuitism"[18] was exactly the pattern of the Culture Christianity found in Ritschl and Harnack,[19] Barth's teachers as well as in his "neo-Protestant" contemporaries who had "Bismarck as their master".[20] Under such terms, Barth emphasized, "theology" for Overbeck was "the Satan of Religion".[21] Christianity become "worldly-wise"[22] was a denial of its basic ascetic character.[23] Having domesticated God for its own purposes, it thought to put God "daily in a bag".[24] A Christianity of this sort was not only worthless to the faith, it was worthless to culture as well.[25] Historical Christianity as thus represented stood in negation to, rather than in continuity with, New Testament faith. There the faith had said "No" to culture. Any faith which resembles that of the New Testament must therefore do the same. It must shout "No" to the Christianity of the pre- and immediate post-World War I periods which tried to identify itself with Western culture.

Rather than being too enthusiastic about following Overbeck's directions, to say nothing of thinking that the promised land would be reached tomorrow or the day after if the protest were loud enough, the first thing that must be done, according to Barth, "is actually to begin to wander in the wilderness".[26] In this way, perhaps, theology which goes through the "narrow gate of Overbeck's negation" might learn something of Christoph Blumhardt's (1805–1880) "Ja", which is the other side of Overbeck's "Nein".[27]

Overbeck's "No" to "historical Christianity" and its co-existential culture was corroborated by Barth's interpretation of the Apostle Paul in the Second Edition of his *Commentary on Paul's Epistle to the Romans*. God and the world, he argued, stand in dialectical opposition. "God who sorrows on our behalf [is] God who can only turn Himself from us and say only 'No'".[28] Only the God who contradicts his own name "affirms the course of this world". As such he is "God — God in His wrath".[29] God's wrath, however, is not his "last word".[30] Wrath is not "the true revelation of Him".[31] Nevertheless, God in his wrath is, in fact, "always God against whom we are thrust".[32] As Barth had learned from Blumhardt, God's "No" thus rests on his "Yes", but for now, for the world and for Christianity as a worldly faith, the "No" is the Word.

Kierkegaard's God as Other

As Overbeck prompted Barth to confront and contrast historical Christianity with "biblical faith", so Søren Kierkegaard more than anyone else taught Barth to stress at that time the infinite qualitative difference between eternity and time, the Kingdom of God and the kingdoms of this world, God and humankind. So great is the hiatus between God and man, time and eternity, God and the gods of this world, family, nation, state, Church and fatherland,[33] that infinity itself is inadequate to represent it. Kierkegaard's "otherness" of God, according to Barth, not only confronts but "dissolves" the whole realm of humanity.[34] Such is the "divine artifice" that it can only be "contrasted with the reality of this world and with all its possible improvements". "It is the wholly pre-eminent truth which must not be received as some particular intrusion of direct reality."[35]

God, therefore, as Barth in the light of Kierkegaard understood him, is the God who is over against us, the God who judges us and calls even the best of our efforts into question.

> May we be preserved from the blasphemy of men who "without being terrified and afraid in the presence of God, without the

agony of death which is the birth-pang of faith, without the trembling [as in *Fear and Trembling*] which is the first requirement of adoration, without the panic of the possibility of scandal, hope to have direct knowledge of that which cannot be directly known . . . and do not rather say that He was truly and verily God, because He was beyond our comprehension" (Kierkegaard).[36]

The "infinite qualitative distinction between time and eternity" which Barth adopted from Kierkegaard possessed negative as well as positive significance. "'God is in his heaven, and thou art on earth.'"[37] The need of the hour, therefore, was to measure the Church by an absolute standard. In the light of this standard there was need "not of patience, but of the impatience of the prophets, not of well-mannered pleasantry, but of a grim assault, not of the historian's balanced judgement . . . but of a love of truth which hacks its way through the very backbone of the matter, and then dares to bring an accusation of unrighteousness against every upright man".[38]

Dostoevski's Ambiguity

Compared with Kierkegaard, Dostoevski was somewhat less strident, more sympathetic with the human condition, more keenly aware of the equivocality of existence. Dostoevski, whom Barth learned to take seriously from his friend, Eduard Thurneysen (1888–1974),[39] taught Barth to see "the impenetrable ambiguity of human life — even of the life of the Christian and of the Christian community".[40] Thus, all we know and are — "our concrete status in the world of time and of men and of things lies under the shadow of death"[41] — even the most miserable of lives are recipients of God's grace. Dialectically, therefore, even depraved createdness is to be understood "as bearing witness to the Creator". What is visible in men as "void and deprivation" is to be seen as "longing and hope for that which is invisible".[42] Ivan Karamazov illustrated the *totaliter aliter* [totally other] predication of our unknown existence in God, the new man, which he is not but who nevertheless dwells in him and who is undeniably his "existential ego".[43]

The man who has once heard the voice and seen the brightness . . . existentially, earnestly, unavoidably, inescapably,
unambiguously, with the eyes and ears of an Ivan Karamazov
himself . . . [is] confronted by the wholly impossible, by the
absolute contradiction, by that which can never be justified and
can never be enthroned in any "concept of God".[44]

In continuity with the above, Dostoevski's Christ figure, the
"Idiot", shows that, "in spite of its supposed richness and
healthiness and righteousness, humanity has no alternative but
death when confronted by the Truth".[45] The Grand Inquisitor
is the supreme illustration of the Church's attempt to "human-
ize the divine, to bring it within the sphere of the world of time
and things, and to make it a practical 'something', for the
benefit of those who cannot live with the Living God and yet
cannot live without God".[46] All such attempts result in "religion". Religion, in turn, gives rise to the religious fanatic
exemplified by the murderer Raskolnikov in *Crime and Pun-
ishment*. Hence, as Raskolnikov illustrates "the possibility of a
final *misunderstanding* of the command that men should fear
and love God above all things",[47] so the Grand Inquisitor
portrays religion's betrayal of Christ as well as our own.[48] The
lesson is obvious; even the Christian, and especially the Christian, stands in the position of the Brothers Karamazov "where
all these evil things are possible".[49]

Let simple minded Occidentals (!) retain such [religious] opin-
ions as long as they are able. But religion is an abyss: it is terror.
There demons appear (Ivan Karamazov and Luther!). There the
old enemy of man is strangely near. There sin deceives. There
the power of the commandment is deadly — *The serpent
beguiled me* (Gen. iii.13).[50]

Such was the structure of Barth's attack on nineteenth-
century liberal theology, on "Christianity" as he knew it, even
in his own patterns of faith.[51] In contrast to the romantic unity
of *faith* and *culture* of his nineteenth-century neo-Protestant
teachers, Barth now pointed to a disjunction, even a contradiction, between the two. God is God and God is holy. Man and
his culture which reflects him are sinful. There is a "qualitative
distinction between God and man and God and the world".[52]
"God is the Holy One, the altogether other."[53] The God of this
world, "the God of Religion" who is synonymous with culture,

is in actuality the "No-God" of this world, the God of wrath.[54] "What is called 'God' is in fact man."[55]

Faith, on the other hand, is in the unknown God.[56] It pronounces a "no" upon this world. Further, it is not the "faith of religion", even of innermost religion, for it "is never identical with 'piety'", no matter how devout.[57] "Depth of feeling [as in Schleiermacher], strength of connection, advance in perception and moral behaviour [as in Ritschl and Herrmann] are no more than things which accompany the birth of faith."[58] As such they are "not positive factors, but negations of other positive factors, stages in the work of clearance". They make room for faith.[59] Faith is contrary to the world. It stands over against the easy belief in progress of the nineteenth-century liberalism in which the world is not only "worshipped and served", but has "become God".[60]

conviction

With Overbeck Barth was convinced that to live in faith is to "live with contradiction".[61] It is to live under the *judgement* of God and this judgement is neither the source nor the sum of power, but "the *krisis* of all power".[62] "'When God makes alive, he kills; when He justifies, He imposes guilt; when He leads us to heaven, He thrusts us down into hell' (Luther)."[63]

Nazi Natural Religion

From a theological perspective World War I must be understood as the outcome of an identification of faith and culture. It was a logical result of a natural theology which, rather than being critical of Church, culture and nation, defended the interrelation and harmony between them. Barth had warned the theological world with his *The Epistle to the Romans* and subsequent writings in the twenties of the dire consequences of the continuing Culture Christianity and had been joined in the effort by friends, among whom were Gogarten and Brunner, especially in the publication of the journal *Zwischen den Zeiten (Between the Times)*. And although students heard him gladly first in Göttingen, then in Münster and lastly in Bonn, from where in 1935 he was escorted by SS troops to the Swiss border and deported, as far as the reigning theologians and churchmen were concerned, there were few ears ready to hear. Rather they, like the German populace in general, looked upon World

War I as a mistake. It was the result of a flaw in the otherwise ongoing positive human and natural development. It was seen as a set-back, a set-back which, in the eyes of the majority of German people, who smarted under the humiliation and terms of the Treaty of Versailles, could be overcome only by a re-establishment of pride and productivity of the German nation, only by a re-assertion of *das Deutsche Volk* (the Germanic people) and its re-ascendance to its "proper place of superiority", at least on the continent of Europe. Little wonder, then, after Germany's ill-fated experiment when the democracy of the Weimar Republic failed and chaos ensued, that the National Socialists (Nazis), who reflected both the frustration of the German people with their subordinate status among the nations and promised not only delivery from humility but renewed glory, were *elected* to power in March 1933.

The Nazi movement, which became a power to be reckoned within the early thirties and which capitalized on Hegel's identity of *Geist* (spirit) and *Volk, Volk* and nation, represented a continued and even accentuated stage of the theological-cultural development against which Barth and his friends had warned. Natural theology at its best was thus theology at its worst. The God of blood and soil, *Volk* and *Altar,* who was worshipped with enthusiasm and who demanded and received unquestioned loyalty and self-sacrifice, was revived. His cross was the *Hakenkreuz* (the swastika). The No-God of the Bible became the Yes-God of the people. The number of child sacrifices demanded by ancient Phoenician and Ammonite Moloch was small in comparison to what was now voraciously demanded by this god's new manifestation.

Against this teutonic brand of natural theology with its emphasis on reading God both off creation and the history of the Germanic peoples, Barth raised his voice in vigorous protest. Against this theology so trenchant and appealing to all that was considered right, honourable, promising, loyal, patriotic and obligatory that it pulled a goodly proportion of the German Church in its wake, *die Bekennende Kirche* (The Confessing Church) [64] was formed and Barth was instrumental in its founding.

Soon after Adolf Hitler (1889–1945) came to power on March 11, 1933, the *German Christians,* a movement within the German Church, began to assert itself. The movement supported the National Socialist or Nazi myth of Aryan social dominance with a mystical identity of blood and nation,[65] with its own myth of a German national religion. It was a religion of the human spirit. It claimed with Nietzsche that the Judaeo-Christian Creator, Father God, was dead. According to the German Christian thinking as represented by Ernest Bergmann (1881–1945) the traditional belief in a "Man God" had to be replaced by the "Great Mother".[66] "God must have a bi-sexual character".[67] The effort, which was aided and abetted, sometimes with a great deal of theological sophistication, by such writers as Emanuel Hirsch, Friedrich Gogarten, W. Stapel and J. Hossenfelder,[68] demanded the formation of a *Reichskirche* (a national Church) which would help to unify the German people by uniting the Protestant Churches under a single Reichsbishop.

By their appeal to the unity of *Thron* and *Altar, Volk* and *Religion,* and with the help given by the presence of Nazi personnel at the polls, the "German Christians" swept the Church elections of July 23, 1933. Then on September 27, 1933, The National Synod, dominated as it was by representatives sympathetic to the Nazi cause, elected Bishop Ludwig Müller (1883–1945), who was chief of the German Army Chaplains and a friend of Hitler, to the office of Reichsbishop. The Synod then proceeded to adopt policies which sought to deprecate the position of the Old Testament as Holy Scripture and extended its anti-semitic convictions by moving to eliminate the term "Israel" from the Church's hymnody and liturgy. Even more portentous, in the short term at least, the Synod adopted as part of the Church's constitution the "Aryan Paragraph" from the new National Constitution which deprived Jews of their citizenship. As Church policy the paragraph excluded pastors of Jewish extraction from the ministry. As Reichsbishop Müller candidly explained, "Equality before God does not include equality before men".[69]

Protest and counter-action were not, however, long in coming. In response to the Nazi-dominated church elections of July 23, 1933, and the ensuing "German Christian" policies, Martin Niemöller (1892–   ), who was later to be rewarded for his anti-Nazi stance by being arrested and spending seven years in the Nazi concentration camps of Sachsenhausen and Dachau, was instrumental in establishing "The Pastors' Emergency League". The 3,000 pastors of the league who claimed as their motto the words "We must obey God rather than men" (Acts 5:29), openly declared their opposition to the elections of July 23 and called the office and authority of the Reichsbishop into question. On November 15, 1933, Barth, who by then was teaching in Bonn, was asked to come to Berlin-Dahlem to meet with the League's leaders. In a statement entitled *Kirchliche Opposition 1933,* which he later admitted he had drawn up in a "great hurry", Barth put before the League leaders in succinct form the terms on which the ensuing "Church struggle" was to be carried out. Basing his thought on the Bible and the Reformation, Barth called for the independence of the Church from state control. If the Church were to remain true to itself it could not allow itself to knuckle under the Nazi-dominated, Nazi-sympathetic German Christian movement. Even more fundamentally however, Barth pointed out — and this is the abiding value of the document — that the struggle was not simply a contest between ecclesiastical parties. At base it was a struggle between theologies.

The conflict was between a theology which was grounded upon the Word of God as witnessed to in Scripture and a naturalistic theology rooted in Meister Eckhart's (*c.* 1260–1328) mystical "God of the Soul", a theology elaborated by Alfred Rosenberg in his *Der Mythos des zwanzigsten Jahrhunderts (The Myth of the Twentieth Century).*[70] This God, Rosenberg explained, is an immanent, creative power calling for heroic action outwardly and mystic harmony inwardly. He is the God of Goethe, "the greatest of modern Germans".[71] This creative God who demands heroic endeavour from his followers and is immanent in the historical process must therefore replace the transcendent and foreign Jewish Jehovah. Such a God calls forth the kind of Confession of Faith proposed by Ernst Bergmann:

> I believe in the God of the German religion who is at work in nature, in the lofty human spirit, and in the strength of his people. I believe in the helper, Christ, who is struggling for the noble human soul. I believe in Germany, the land of culture for a new humanity.[72]

The god of nature and natural theology had again come alive and Barth recognized him and called him by name.

Barth's Confessional Stance

Ecclesiastical opposition inspired by the kind of theology Barth had proclaimed in Berlin-Dahlem against the official Nazi-inspired *Reichskirche* (National Church) not only began to grow among individual Christians, it began to form itself into a movement of Churches against the Nazi-dominated ecclesiastical structure. On January 3–4, 1934, the first Confessional Synod of the Reformed (Calvinistic) Evangelical Church met in Barmen. Again Barth submitted a theological statement similar to the one he had written for the meeting in Berlin-Dahlem some six weeks previously. The statement in which Barth elaborated the Reformed doctrine of the Church was adopted by the Synod as its confession and became the model of Church-state relationships on the basis of which the whole theological and ecclesiastical opposition to the Nazis was to take place.

The confession identified the Church-state alliance of the German Christians, while characterizing it as "The Church of the Pope". In contrast to the German Christian dependence on natural theology and nationalism, the statement proclaimed that the Church was founded on the revelation of the Word of God according to the witness of Scripture. Word and sacrament alone regulate the Church and the lives of its members whether in relation to *Volk,* state or culture. The promise of Christ and his Word alone govern the Church's outward order and its inner life. Practically, therefore, the Church alone must determine its own leadership without outside interference.

The state, too, was acknowledged to have its proper place. The Church, in fact, which is one throughout the ages, "recognizes in the state a divine order". Therefore the state, no less than the Church, is responsible to "the Lord of Lords". Hence the state can no more be replaced by the Church than it can determine what the Church's message should be. Just as the Church is free under her divine order, so "the state is free in accomplishing its task".[73]

The Confessing anti-Nazi Church movement continued to

gain strength with the result that some three and a half months later, on April 22, 1934, representatives from the different Provincial Churches which refused to submit to Hitler's Reichsbishop Müller and the Nazi sympathetic German Christian Movement, met at Ulm. They accused the Reichsbishop of illegal action in having declared that the German churches were under his control. In order to counter the Reichsbishop the representatives proclaimed that the newly constituted *Confessing Church* was the constitutional Evangelical Church of Germany. On May 23, 1934, thirty-five professors, among them Barth and Bultmann, signed a public declaration asserting the freedom of the Church from the domination and control of the state and thus added to the momentum of the Confessing Church movement which stood in direct opposition to the "German Christians".

Then, on May 29–31, 1934, The First Confessing Synod of the German Evangelical [Protestant] Church met at Barmen[74] and issued its *Magna Carta, The Barmen Declaration*. The original draft of the declaration which was written by Barth, was a re-emphasis on and an expansion of the position set out by the statement which Barth had presented to the leaders of the Pastors' Emergency League in November 1933 and to the Reformed Church Synod at Barmen in January 1934. The document is Christocentric and Bible-centred and, as one might have expected, it demands a clear division between the responsibilities of Church and state. "Jesus Christ as he is attested for us in Holy Scripture" is proclaimed as "the one Word of God which we have to hear and which we have to trust and obey in life and in death".[75] Speaking specifically to the situation, the declaration stated:

> We reject the false doctrine, as though the Church could and would have to acknowledge as a source of its proclamation, apart from and besides this one Word of God, still other events and powers, figures and truths, as God's revelation.[76]

The Confession was a re-emphasis, then, on the centrality of faith as represented by the Old and New Testaments as over against this final brand of Culture-Christianity, i.e., a natural theology run wild. The false doctrine intimating that there are areas of life which do not belong to Jesus Christ, but to other lords, was rejected.[77] Rejected, too, were the doctrines: that the Church could abandon the form of its message in favour of "prevailing ideological and political connections";[78] that "special leaders vested with ruling powers" could be imposed upon the Church;[79] that the state could become a totalitarian order over life in general; and that the Church should either take on the tasks of the state or become an organ of it.[80] Finally, "We reject the false doctrine, as though the Church in human arrogance could place the Word and work of the Lord in the service of any arbitrarily chosen desires, purposes and plans".[81] In sum, Culture-Christianity along with all "natural theology" on which it is based was repudiated in unequivocal terms.

In that Barth had already made his position so clear in November 1933, the whole *Confessing Movement* could be seen as an extension of his mind into the Church at large or at least into that part of it which was given "ears to hear".

Of all the statements, "the small memorandum" which Barth put together in a "flying rush" and which, as mentioned above, was on November 15, 1933 presented to the leadership of the *Pastors' Emergency League* meeting in Berlin-Dahlem, is perhaps most penetrating in its theological analysis.[82] In the statement entitled *Church Opposition 1933,* Barth pointed out first that the protest was in opposition both to "the *false teaching*" as well as to "the usurpation" of the Church's doctrine by the German Christians. However, and in the light of our discussion of extreme importance, Barth then went on to show that the German Christian disease was a malaise of the Church at large.

> Because the teaching and attitude of the German Christians is nothing else than an especially powerful result of the whole neo-Protestant [nineteenth-century Protestant liberal] development since 1700, the protest directs itself against a pernicious and obvious corruption of the whole evangelical [Protestant] Church.
>
> The gist of the matter is as follows: The protest against the false teaching of the German Christians cannot first begin with the Aryan paragraph, the rejection of the Old Testament, the Arianism of the German-Christian Christology, the naturalism and Pelagianism of the German-Christian doctrines of justification and sanctification, the idolization of the state in the German-Christian ethics. It must fundamentally direct itself

against the fact (as against the source of all individual errors) that the German Christians, besides Holy Scripture as the unique source of revelation, affirm the German nationhood, its history and its present political actuality as a second source of revelation and thereby betray themselves as believers in "another God".[83]

"Nein" to Brunner's Natural Theology

Barth's basic protest, then, was against natural theology as such, and it was on this basis that the whole Confessing Church movement against the Nazi-dominated German Christian Church and eventually against the totalitarian, inhuman and genuinely pernicious policies of the Nazi regime was grounded. As the future unfolded it was the impetus of the Confessing Church, though it did not remain as strong as Barth for one desired, which held aloft a flicker of hope even in the most dire of times. When the war ended this same impulse became the foundation for the renewal and revitalization of the German Church leading it to its "Stuttgart Confession" and its re-integration as the Evangelical Church of Germany into the ecumenical movement.

In retrospect, therefore, it is rather easy to understand Barth's utter exasperation with his old friend and one-time comrade in the "dialectical theological movement", fellow Swiss Reformed theologian Emil Brunner (1889–1966) for trying to revive the subject of natural theology.[84] It was in the midst of the crisis with the German Christians in 1934 that Brunner wrote his *Natur und Gnade (Nature and Grace)*. In the pamphlet he took Barth to task for his opposition to natural theology, and proposed an "enlightened natural theology" which he was convinced was justified both by the Scripture and by the Reformation.[85]

Barth's answer was his famous *Nein! Antwort an Emil Brunner (No! Answer to Emil Brunner)* delivered in not always modulated tones, but laying bare the fact that the basis of Brunner's misunderstanding of the faith was identical with that which was at the time leading the German Christians astray and was allowing them to ally themselves with the Nazi cause.[86] In a second edition of his work issued in 1935[87] Brunner added a "Preface" which affirmed his specific rejection of the German Christian position on the grounds that it misused the Bible and pronounced clear biblical doctrines to be heretical. Brunner, however, found no coincidence between the position of the German Christians and his own, nor did he understand the German Christian position to be the result of "natural theology" as such.[88]

For Barth, however, the confrontation with Brunner revealed exactly what was at stake. Barth was fully aware of Brunner's "good intentions". They were, as a fact, identical to those of Schleiermacher whose famous book which had advocated a form of Culture-Christianity a hundred and thirty-five years previously had been appropriately entitled *Religion: Speeches to Its Cultured Despisers*. Thus, according to Barth, Brunner with his "enlightened natural theology", "wishes to carry on pastoral work among intellectuals, to instruct modern youth, to carry on discussion with the unbelievers".[89] Brunner wanted to apologize for the faith, if not to its intellectual despisers, then to those who were indifferent to the faith and to whom the world was real but for whom faith, at least in its traditional form, had no relevance.[90]

Brunner's intentions were not to be despised since they overlapped with Barth's own. "It is necessary", Brunner wrote, "for a Christian *theologia naturalis*", i.e., "for Christian theological thinking which tries to account for the phenomena of rational life".[91] Rather than move with the possibilities which might have been offered by modern Einsteinian and quantum physical science, however, Brunner returned to the Thomistic and Aristotelian thesis which, as we have seen, was the thesis of the post-seventeenth-century "Newtonian theologians". "Wherever God does anything, he leaves the imprint of his nature upon what he does."[92] Thus the creation of the world was regarded at the same time as a revelation. It was self-communication of God.[93] With that Brunner was not only back with Newton and the natural theologians who followed him and who had considered themselves capable of reading God off the universe, but he also adopted the idealistically informed Enlightenment position of claiming for man "a point of contact" *(Anknüpfungspunkt)* which he defined as man's *"capacity* for words and responsibility".[94]

The Word of God does not have to create man's capacity for words. He has never lost it, it is the presupposition of his ability to hear the Word of God. But the Word of God itself creates man's ability to believe the Word of God, i.e., the ability to hear it in *such a way* as is only possible in the faith.[95]

Thus, for Brunner, not only Roman Catholic theology but all theology rests on the *analogia entis* (analogy of being), a likeness of being in man to God himself.[96] The *imago Dei,* "man's undestroyed formal likeness to God", therefore provided "the *objective possibility* for the revelation of God in his 'Word'".[97]

Barth's rejection of Brunner's argument was a warning to all who, like myself, would take nature as nature (and science as defining nature) more seriously than does Barth himself. Barth pointed to the danger of being caught in the very Thomism which had to be broken before modern science could develop.[98] But he also pointed to the equally disastrous plight of neo-Protestantism, i.e., nineteenth-century liberalism which arose through Kant on the back of seventeenth-century science and considered itself faithful to it.

Since the problem here is complex, it is rather important to realise that, when considering the relationship of nature and grace, the positions of Thomism and neo-Protestantism are simply two sides of the same coin. Both depend on human natural ability by and of itself to understand God. As Barth pointed out, the Thomist principle of *gratia non tollit sed praesupponit et perficit naturam* (grace does not destroy but presupposes and perfects nature)[99] found its mature form via the Reformers' appeal to Augustine (354–430) in Schleiermacher's *The Christian Faith*. From there it became "part of the armoury of modernist Protestantism".[100]

As far as Barth was concerned, Brunner's primary error lay in the fact that he forgot the radical character of "the fall" and the consequent ambiguity of nature. Thus Brunner evoked quite simply and directly the "original creation so far as it is still recognizable as such". He attempted to see "the God-given form of all created being", and also "the will of God imprinted upon all existence from creation". In this scheme man's "experience" of God's "preserving and providential grace" was understood to be "an important complement to the

knowledge of God derived from Scripture". The system conceived of a hidden *lex naturae* (natural law) which merely needs
to be brought out into the open again through the help of
Scripture, i.e., what Brunner called the "ordinances of creation
and nature that have only been somewhat obscured by sin".
Obscured, too, were "the *humanum*" and finally "the rational
nature of man as the *imago dei*" (image of God),[101] which
require similar treatment.

Barth's critique was not entirely negative. He agreed with
Brunner in asking the double question, "*What* has to be done?
How is it to be done?" The first question concerned "content",
the second concerned "language".[102] For Barth, however, the
questions of method, language and form were not to be separated from that of content. Theology is not a "matter of
abstraction". And whoever makes of it an "abstraction" will
inevitably be caught in some kind of natural theology.[103] The
question "How?", therefore, must always be included in the
question "What?"[104]

Brunner's attempt was to produce "an enlightened natural
theology" which in some way or other is dependent on human
ability to understand God by way of an innate faculty *independent* of God's gracious intervention with man in that process of
understanding. For Barth this was to fly in the face of the
Reformation doctrines expressing the theme of the sovereignty
of God and especially of John Calvin's (1509–1564) emphasis
on the necessity of grace for understanding as well as for
salvation. As Calvin himself put it:

> But although the Lord represents both himself and his everlast-
> ing Kingdom in the mirror of his works with very great clarity,
> such is our stupidity that we grow increasingly dull toward so
> manifest testimonies, and they flow away without profiting us.[105]
> Therefore, since either the custom of the city or the agreement
> of tradition is too weak and frail a bond of piety to follow in
> worshipping God, it remains for God himself to give witness of
> himself from heaven.[106]

Faith and Faith "Alone"?

Having handed the palm to Barth, the reader will, no doubt,
have formed the opinion that I am a somewhat too uncritical

Barthian. Though I am happy to regard him as one of my teachers, I would also want to be counted as one who identifies with Barth in his own statement, "If there are Barthians, then I am not one of them".[107] In this context my question with regard to Barth has to do with his persistent neglect of natural science and what that neglect may have meant for his theological concepts including his theological language. Certainly, it is true as Barth maintained, that the question "How?" must always include the question "What?". In other words, the method of inquiry must fit the object of inquiry.

The question is, however, if Barth who knew very well that the Gospel, to be the Gospel, must be good news for today, reckoned seriously enough with the influence of natural science upon today's world and its understanding. It is all very well to insist that the theological science which has its own particular object must be unique because its object is unique. However, since theology, as Barth was perfectly willing to admit, belongs to the created order — like the Bible it does not fall from heaven[108] — we must ask whether the concepts of all sciences, in this case natural science and theological science, do not necessarily bear upon one another? Hence to imply, as does Edmund Schlink (1903–), that theology has to do with the scientist but not with science itself,[109] or with Barth that there is free scope for natural science beyond what theology describes as the work of the Creator,[110] appears to place theology (thoughts and statements with reference to God) in our day in the kind of insulated solitude where it has never been and by the nature of both its finitude and cultural integration can never be. God is transcendent but our thoughts and statements about him are not. Although theology does not derive from nature, and hence is not "natural theology", it nevertheless partakes of nature and is necessarily expressed in terms of this world.

This has implications, of course, for the Scriptures themselves. Just as the theologies of the Old Testament cannot be understood outside the contextual influences of Semitic culture in general, so the different theological understandings and specifically the different Christological emphases of the New Testament are to be explained as arising within the milieu of Palestinian-Jewish, Hellenistic-Jewish and Hellenistic-

Gentile thought within which the Christian faith itself arose.[111] Though this thought was essentially "a-scientific" the cosmologies which are present had a definite influence on the terms used to express the Gospel. The analysis is also relevant to post-New Testament conciliar decisions with regard to Christology and the doctrine of the Trinity. Here especially Platonic and neo-Platonic philosophical concepts, which were integrated with contemporary physics, played their part and must be clarified if the doctrines are to be understood.[112] Thus, any epistemological détente between theology and the other sciences simply will not do.

On the other hand, it would seem quite illegitimate to cite Bernhard Bavink against Barth as does Herbert Meschkowski who, like myself, pleads for the necessity of dialogue between science and theology in our time.

> *The Barthian solely transcendent God is a pure theologoumenon so conceived that a closed theological system can be worked out accordingly.* The real God, however, is not confined by the fences and boundaries which even the apparently most pious and most consistent theologians set out: He works where, how, when and through that which He will.[113]

Barth saw only too clearly what the neo-Protestant God of natural theology, which was indeed a *theologoumenon* based on idealistic subjectivistic Enlightenment concepts, could do to the Church, culture, and state alike. Barth's God was not solely transcendent, nor did Barth deny that God may reveal himself "where, how, when and through that which He will". However, having known a good number of theologians who were certain that God had revealed himself through the German *Volk,* the German culture and the German nation as well as through the Führer himself, it is quite understandable that he should insist that the doctrines and practice of the church be consistent with the teaching which had allowed the Church to remain faithful in the past. It was because Barth was convinced that the particularity of the faith is essential that he, like the Reformers of the sixteenth century, reached back to the formula *solus Christus* (Christ alone), as witnessed to in the Church on the basis of *sola scriptura* (Scripture alone)[114] as the sure foundation of theological discourse.

Barth's position may well be inadequate because he did not

make the effort to reckon with modern science as Meschkowski and I, too, would prefer. But to take Barth to task for not appreciating "natural theology" and to classify his doctrine of God as a "*theologoumenon*" is simply to misunderstand the deep and eventually faith-destroying consequences which Brunner's and similar attempts to resurrect a *theologia naturalis* involve.[115] More specifically, it is to overlook the complexity of the theological state of affairs in the early nineteen thirties within which and over against which Barth's concept of the *otherness of God,* who at one and the same time is *far from* and *near to* his creation, but in no sense to be confused with it, was worked out.

Thus, although Barth recognized full well that the God who "works how, when, and through that which He will" cannot be "confined by fences and boundaries", to refer back to Meschkowski's expressions, he did tend to spell out the "where", "how", "when", and "through which" in biblical, especially Pauline, New Testament concepts, and not least as they were developed by the councils of Nicea, Constantinople and Chalcedon. Barth knew, of course, that if theology is to have any standard of validity, it must be measured in terms of continuity with the theological concepts of the past and especially with the witness of the Old and New Testaments. Only in this way will the Church today, like the people of the Old and New Testaments and the early post-New Testament Church in their day, have criteria by which it can differentiate what is legitimate from what is not, what is "true" from what is "false".[116] Thus the Apostle Paul could say, "Even if we, or an angel from heaven, should preach to you a gospel contrary to that which we preached to you, let him be accursed" (Gal. 1:8).

Though even a cursory reading of Barth shows his profound respect and appreciation of culture and its attendant intellectual developments, it is also true that he was convinced of the power of the faith over any system of current thought whatsoever:

> Christian faith is an element which, when it is mingled with philosophies, makes itself felt even in the most diluted forms, and that in a way which is disturbing, destructive and threatening to the very foundations of these philosophies. To the extent that it is faith in God's Word, and is even partially true to itself,

it cannot become faith in current world-views, but can only resist them.[117]

In a real sense the first sentence of this statement can be interpreted as showing that faith has little to fear from mingling with philosophy, science or whatever. The faith, however, must remain faith in God who is continually beyond the confines of any conceptuality (including those of theology) but who must empower any of them if they are to begin to approximate becoming the ways by which he himself makes himself known. On the other hand, the second sentence is a dire warning against the subtle substitution of any philosophical conceptuality, no matter how sophisticated, for those which are proper to the realities of faith itself.[118]

That having been said, however, it must also be pointed out that since faith has no language of its own it must *ipso facto* adopt some language or other, and inevitably this language will reflect world-views that are not entirely appropriate to the Christian faith and in particular instances may well be contrary to it. All languages prove to be inadequate, and all expressions of faith are more or less fallacious. They remain appropriate as long and only as long as they become conduits for the content of faith. They become inadequate just as soon as they become *containers* of it. The somewhat frightening aspect of this matter is that language and concepts which at one time may have proven adequate to the faith may continue to be *de rigueur* in spite of their possible irrelevance. When this happens, when the world moves beyond the *Sitz im Leben* of a language, faith couched in its terms is itself apt to be judged irrelevant. On the other hand, as we have seen, it is often the case that modes of thought and expression may arise which, when used to express the faith within their own terms, limit or distort it beyond recognition.

Such was the case, in fact, with nineteenth-century liberalism toward which Barth directed the barrage of his *The Epistle to the Romans,* which marked the beginning of the end of the easy, optimistic, humanistic, culture-centered liberalism of nineteenth-century theology:

> Paul, as a child of his age, addressed his contemporaries. It is, however, far more important that, as Prophet and Apostle of the Kingdom of God, he veritably speaks to all men of every age.

The differences between then and now, there and here, no doubt require careful investigation and consideration. But the purpose of such investigation can only be to demonstrate that these differences are, in fact, purely trivial. The historical-critical method of Biblical investigation has its rightful place: it is concerned with the preparation of the intelligence — and this can never be superfluous. But, were I driven to choose between it and the venerable doctrine of Inspiration, I should without hesitation adopt the latter, which has a broader, deeper, more important justification. The doctrine of Inspiration is concerned with the labour of apprehending, without which no technical equipment, however complete, is of any use whatever. Fortunately, I am not compelled to choose between the two. Nevertheless, my whole energy of interpreting has been expended in an endeavour to see through and beyond history into the spirit of the Bible, which is the Eternal Spirit. What was once of grave importance, is so still. What is today of grave importance — and not merely crotchety and incidental — stands in direct connexion with that ancient gravity. If we rightly understand ourselves, our problems are the problems of Paul; and if we be enlightened by the brightness of his answers, those answers must be ours.[119]

Questioning the Categories

It is no doubt true, as Barth put it, that: "What was once of grave importance, is so still. What is today of grave importance . . . stands in direct connexion with that ancient gravity".[120] But it is also true that, unless we want to rely on some kind of Kantian, Schleiermacherian or Herrmannian *private intuition, feeling* or *inwardness,* we can only discern "what was once of grave importance" by utilizing the scientific method of inquiry. We may discern the relationship between "what was once of grave importance" and "what is of grave importance today" only with proper attention to methods of thought and logic which are nowhere scripturally designated or defined. The different New Testament writers appear to have emphasized different aspects of the faith as being most important, changing them to suit the purpose of propagating the faith in their own situations. Likewise, in our day different situations may require different "gospels" for *the Gospel* to be proclaimed.[121] If so, just as modern science had to re-assess the categories of Plato and Aristotle in order to become free for its own development, so theology, too, must continually re-appraise the terms in which its doctrine is delivered if it is to be free to develop as it should.

There is no doubt grave danger in any "category change", but to cite Günter Howe again, "Consciously or unconsciously all theological discourse is bound to use the terms of contemporary thought".[122] Therefore, the greater danger would seem to be absolute insistence upon known theological terminology with the rather naïve presumption that the concepts once formulated *ipso facto* express the same content today which they did at the time of their formulation. They may, but they may not. Theological responsibility would seem to demand accountability in this regard.

Barth, like Howe, knew full well that theology has no other language than that of the culture in which the Church finds itself. That being the case, it would seem extremely doubtful whether in a scientific technological age, such as is the one in which we find ourselves, any "free scope" for natural science outside of theology can exist which has no relevance for theology or whether any relevant theology can exist without affecting science. It would seem more likely, since science and technology exert tremendous influence on both our lives and our concepts of thought that they modify one another. Thus, whether we like it or not, the question for theology is, "How does or should science and technology affect theology and how does or should theology affect science and technology?" Only if we are conscious of the interpretation of the "sciences", the natural sciences and the human sciences including theology, will we be responsible for their mutual development.

In sum, as Jews and Christians have always lived in the world, so their concepts, even their theological concepts, have been influenced by the thought structures of that world. It will hardly do for us to point to Canaanite, Babylonian and Persian influences in the Old Testament and the Jewish apocalyptic, Alexandrian philosophical, Hellenistic and emperor cult influences in the New Testament without realizing that we too are influenced by our world. More specifically, we would not be consistent if we were to acknowledge, as we must, the Platonic and neo-Platonic influences in the post-New Testament

Church, a re-emphasis of Plato in Anselm (1033–1109), the importance of Aristotle for Thomas Aquinas, and of Augustine for Luther and Calvin without recognizing that our thought, too, has philosophical foundations. With regard to the investigation of the previous pages, it would not serve our purpose to call attention to the dimension of idealism in Schleiermacher and the nineteenth-century neo-Protestants and the consequences of Heideggerian existentialism in Bultmann and Tillich, and then claim a kind of force-free field for ourselves or anyone else. The question is never whether or not theology is influenced by so-called "non-theological concepts". The only question is, "Are the factors which give shape to theological thought recognized and handled responsibly so that theology is able to use them rather than be used by them?" Hence Hans Urs von Balthasar's (1905–) judgement that Barth was in some measure beholden to neo-Kantian precepts[123] does not necessarily discredit Barth's conceptuality. It does, however, indicate that Barth's thought structures share finitude with all other such structures and are, therefore, only *relatively adequate* in being the means by which the Gospel may be expressed. Who can claim more? More adequate concepts may come to hand, however, if we take seriously the scientific and technological world in which the factors of relativity and quantum physics play an extremely important role.

In this regard it may be time not only to question the intellectual nurseries of Barth which he had very much in common with his nineteenth-century predecessors with whom he had firmly and with good cause disagreed, but it may be time to rechoose our own intellectual ancestors and adopt people like Max Planck (1858–1947), Albert Einstein (1879–1955), Werner Heisenberg (1901–1976), or Niels Bohr (1885–1962).[124] These may prove to be, and I am quite convinced they already are, the "world-view" or "world-concept" makers of our times, just as Socrates, Plato and Aristotle were concept-makers for the world-views of their time. The immense influence that Newton has had on theology, both directly and indirectly through Kant, who idealized the Newtonian concepts of space and time via the *"synthetic a priori"*, would seem like Newtonian physics itself to have run its course and reached a dead end as far as universal conceptuality is concerned.

Karl Barth's theology, which has certainly been constructive
for the twentieth-century Church and proved to be indispensable in the face of the Nazi-influenced German Christian
movement of the early thirties, continues to stand head and
shoulders above any of its purported alternatives simply
because Barth insists on expressing God as transcendent as
well as immanent, the eternal mystery who makes himself
known to us when, where and how he will in the community of
believers. Nevertheless, as we shall see shortly, Barth's
theology, as he would be the first to admit, may not be the last
word. In particular his hesitation to admit the relevance of the
new advances in natural science and physics in particular for
theological articulation actually meant that he failed to take
advantage of conversations with some of the leading scientists
after World War II. Rather, he continued lecturing on and
putting into print his massive and, for theological scholarship
quite indispensable, *Church Dogmatics* very much as if men
such as Planck, Einstein, de Broglie, Heisenberg and Bohr had
not lived or discovered anything that could possibly challenge,
concur with or re-orient the terms in which faith should be
expressed. Such theologians as S. L. Jaki and T. F. Torrance
are forcing us to realize, however, that it will not do to remain
content with such a hiatus between Christian theology and
natural science. We now have opportunity to follow their lead.

For all his genius Barth's epistemological teaching, at least as
far as its terminology was concerned, remained rooted by and
large in the conceptuality which arose before the age of the
sciences which have redefined our understanding of the created
world. Barth stressed over and over again the "proclaimed
Word" *today* as the "first form" of the Word of God, the mode
by which we, in fact, hear the Word today. However, when that
Word is expressed rather exclusively in thought-constructs
deriving from the human sciences, one is led to ask if the
categories of any particular philosophical or scientific era are
final for the expression of faith. Are they, for instance, any
more final for theology than Ptolemaic, Copernican or even
Einsteinian science for cosmology? Ptolemy, as we know from
Einsteinian relativity, was not necessarily wrong in following
Plato and Aristotle's geocentricity rather than adopting the
heliocentricity of Aristarchus of Samos. His system of circles

within circles with the earth in the centre, the sun, moon, the planets orbiting around it, making weird configurations following cycles and epicycles, so that their apparent "irregular motion" could be explained, was not necessarily wrong. It agrees, in fact, with what was considered to be competent observation and made sense for some 1500 years. Nevertheless the system was so complicated, so spirit-filled and so subject to the constant intervention of a deity for "order" to be preserved, that when a simpler, more harmonious system began to inform observation, the old system simply stretched scientifically informed credibility to the breaking point.

The order of the solar system has, of course, remained much the same for the last two thousand years or for the last several million years, for that matter.[125] Our understanding, our conceptions and perceptions of it have, however, undergone what is legitimately and paradigmatically called "a Copernican revolution". In the same sense, it may seem at least possible, therefore, that though God remains God, just as the universe remains the universe, the concepts of faith too may undergo "Copernican revolutions". They need not necessarily be of the Kantian kind where thorough-going "subjectivity" replaces equally thorough-going "objectivity". What one may perhaps hope for in this regard is a theology which takes the present view of created reality, as offered us by modern science, so seriously that at least some of what we may call the "parochialness of traditional Christian faith" may be broken. If so, faith may again be expressed in terms with which the world is conversant. This does not mean, of course, that faith will automatically be understood. It does mean, however, that the "strangeness of faith" may be expressed in a select but current idiom of our time just as the faith of the people of the Old and New Testaments or that of the post-New Testament Church was expressed in selected, current idioms of their times.[126]

The crisis in which we find ourselves in the world would seem to be so serious that attempts by scientists to understand the faith and by theologians to understand science ought to be encouraged on all fronts. The result, as far as theology is concerned, may be a new understanding of reality, together with a re-working of the terms we use, so that we may again be able to grasp it in relation to our "every day world" as a whole.

Here we may hope with Dietrich Bonhoeffer that we may not reserve some space for God apart from life. Rather, we must "speak of God not on the boundaries but at the centre, not in weakness but in strength; and therefore not in death and guilt but in man's life and goodness". "God is beyond in the midst of our life." [127] However, the risk is there, a risk which may cause faith itself to undergo a new reformation and it may be that the "new Christianity", like the original when it encountered the traditional Graeco-Roman religions, will also seem "religion-less". [128]

Getting back to Barth, however, certainly the late Professor Daniel Lamont of the University of Edinburgh, a disciple of Lord Kelvin though not a disciple of Karl Barth, caught the gist of the contribution of even "the early" Barth.

> The significance of Karl Barth in modern thought is that he has reversed the direction in which theology was moving when he found it. There is much in his theological system that is open to criticism, but that is another matter. He has done the biggest thing that a theologian has done since Luther and Calvin. Taking up the line of the prophetic Kierkegaard and the deep-seeing Dostoevsky, he has brought back into the light what should never have been allowed to slip into the shade, that God is neither an object among objects nor a subject among subjects, but *the Subject* of subjects. [129]

Torrance's assessment of Karl Barth in his entirety is thus to the point, "A greater than St Thomas is here". [130]

Footnotes to Chapter IV

1. T. F. Torrance, *Karl Barth, An Introduction to His Early Theology 1910–1931* (London, 1962), p. 33. Cf. Karl Barth, *God, Grace and the Gospel* (Edinburgh, 1959), pp. 56 f.
2. Cf. Torrance, *Karl Barth*, p. 33, n. 1.
3. Barth's father, Fritz, a New Testament scholar who represented the "positive school" and Adolf Schlatter, likewise a Swiss and a New Testament scholar, both left their mark on Barth.
4. Barth, *Protestant Theology*, pp. 129 ff.
5. Karl Barth, *Church Dogmatics* II/1 (Edinburgh, 1957), pp. 632 f. Karl Barth, *Antwort* (Zürich, 1956), p. 840.
6. Harnack was "knighted" becoming Adolf *von* Harnack in 1914.
7. Busch, *Karl Barth*, p. 93.
8. Overbeck's 1873 publication, *Über die Christlichkeit unserer heutigen Theologie,* was an early re-emphasis of the eschatological theme of Reimarus which was later taken up again by Johannes Weiss (1863–1914) and Albert Schweitzer (1875–1965). His *Christentum und Kultur,* subtitled *Gedanken und Anmerkungen zur modernen Theologie (Thoughts and Observations on Modern Theology),* was edited from Overbeck's literary remains by C. A. Berneulli in 1919.
9. Karl Barth, *Die Theologie und die Kirche, Gesammelte Vorträge,* 2 vols. (München, 1928), II, 1-25. Whether or not Barth's lecture interprets Overbeck correctly at all points, as Hans Schindler, *Barth und Overbeck* (Gotha, 1936) indicates it does not, is of secondary import compared to the question of how Barth used Overbeck to express the development of his own thought. Barth, in fact, indicated that it is necessary to read Overbeck's *Christentum und Kultur* "in verschiedenen Richtungen diametral zu lesen, wenn es seine Werkung ausüben will" (in diametrically opposite directions if it is to have its effect"), p. 3. Cf. also, Torrance, *Karl Barth,* pp. 29 ff., for an appraisal of Barth's use of Overbeck's position.
10. Barth, *Theologie und Kirche,* II, 6.
11. Franz Overbeck, *Christentum und Kultur,* edited by C. A. Berneulli (Basel, 1919), p. 247.
12. *Ibid.,* p. 242.
13. *Ibid.,* p. 28.
14. *Ibid.,* p. 54.
15. *Ibid.,* p. 74.
16. Barth, *Theologie und Kirche,* II, 13. This would seem to be Barth's earliest statement referring to Christianity as a non-religion, a designation often thought to be original with Bonhoeffer. Overbeck would seem to have adopted the non-religion category of faith from his friend, Heinrich von Treitschke. Cf. Schindler, *Barth und Overbeck,* pp. 9-11, 16-17.
17. Overbeck, *Christentum,* p. 63.
18. *Ibid.,* pp. 123-25.
19. Barth, *Theologie und Kirche,* II, 19.
20. Overbeck, *Christentum,* p. 155.
21. Barth, *Theologie und Kirche,* II, 20.

146   THEOLOGY AND SCIENCE IN MUTUAL MODIFICATION

22. *Ibid.*
23. *Ibid.*
24. Overbeck, *Christentum,* p. 268.
25. Barth, *Theologie und Kirche,* pp. 21 f.
26. *Ibid.,* p. 24.
27. *Ibid.,* p. 25.
28. Karl Barth, *The Epistle to the Romans* (translated from the Sixth Edition by Edwyn Hoskins, 1933: London, 1950), p. 43. Cf. Karl Barth, *Der Römerbrief* (München, 1929), p. 19.
29. Barth, *Romans,* p. 43; *Römerbrief,* p. 19.
30. *Ibid.*
31. *Ibid.*
32. *Ibid.*
33. Barth, *Romans,* p. 50; *Römerbrief,* p. 26.
34. Barth, *Romans,* p. 278; *Römerbrief,* p. 262.
25. Barth, *Romans,* p. 279; *Römerbrief,* p. 262, citing Kierkegaard.
36. *Ibid.*
37. Barth, *Romans,* p. 10; *Römerbrief,* "Vorwort zur zweiten Auflage".
38. Barth, *Romans,* p. 395; *Römerbrief,* p. 380.
39. Barth, *Antwort,* p. 863.
40. Barth, *Romans,* p. 505; *Römerbrief,* p. 489.
41. Barth, *Romans,* p. 238; *Römerbrief,* p. 220.
42. Barth, *Romans,* p. 122; *Römerbrief,* p. 116.
43. Barth, *Romans,* p. 299; *Römerbrief,* p. 283.
44. Barth, *Romans,* p. 299-300; *Römerbrief,* p. 283.
45. Barth, *Romans,* p. 354; *Römerbrief,* p. 339.
46. Barth, *Romans,* p. 332; *Römerbrief,* p. 317.
47. Barth, *Romans,* p. 356; *Römerbrief,* p. 340. Italics added.
48. Barth, *Romans,* p. 393; *Römerbrief,* p. 378.
49. Barth, *Romans,* p. 501; *Römerbrief,* p. 485. "God is pure negation; He is both 'here' and 'there'. He is the negation of the negation in which the other world contradicts this world and this world, the other world. He is the death of our death and the non-existence of our non-existence." Barth, *Romans,* pp. 141 f.; *Römerbrief,* pp. 123 f. God is the unknown, the hidden God. Barth, *Romans,* p. 505; *Römerbrief,* p. 488. God is the "crisis" of God, "Against? Yes, because — For!" Barth, *Romans,* p. 504; *Römerbrief,* p. 488.
50. Barth, *Romans,* p. 253; *Römerbrief,* p. 235.
51. Cf. T. F. Torrance's comment in *Karl Barth, An Introduction to His Early Theology* where he cites Karl Adam's statement that *The Commentary on Romans* was the bomb that exploded "on the playground of the theologians" p. 17. In his lectures on Dogmatics at the University of Edinburgh, Professor Torrance added, "Like a real bomb, the *Römerbrief* also blew itself up in the explosion". From my lecture notes of the academic year 1953–1954.
52. Barth, *Romans,* p. 39; *Römerbrief,* p. 14.
53. Barth, *Romans,* p. 42; *Römerbrief,* p. 18.
54. Barth, *Romans,* p. 43; *Römerbrief,* p. 19.

55. Barth, *Romans,* p. 44; *Römerbrief,* p. 20.
56. Barth, *Romans,* p. 40; *Römerbrief,* p. 15.
57. *Ibid.*
58. Barth, *Romans,* p. 39; *Römerbrief,* p. 14.
59. *Ibid.*
60. Barth, *Romans,* p. 52; *Römerbrief,* p. 28.
61. Barth, *Romans,* p. 39; *Römerbrief,* p. 14.
62. Barth, *Romans,* p. 36; *Römerbrief,* p. 11.
63. Barth, *Romans,* p. 39; *Römerbrief,* p. 14.
64. For a full account of the matter, cf. Karl Barth, "Zum Kirchenkampf", *Theologische Existenz Heute,* Neue Folge (München, 1956). Cf. also Adolf Keller, *Religion and the European Mind* (London, 1934), published in the U.S.A. as *Religion and Revelation,* and T. H. L. Parker, *Karl Barth: The German Church in Conflict* (London, 1965).
65. Cf. Alfred Rosenberg, *Der Mythos des zwanzigsten Jahrhunderts* (München, 1935).
66. Keller, *Religion,* p. 109.
67. *Ibid.*
68. E. Hirsch, *Das kirchliche Wollen der deutschen Christen* (Berlin, 1933); F. Gogarten, *Politische Ethik* (Jena, 1933); W. Stapel, *Der christliche Staatsmann* (Hamburg, 1933). The list is all the more significant because Hirsch was on the faculty at Göttingen with Barth. Gogarten, also later of Göttingen, was a friend of Barth in the early "dialectical theology" era.
69. Keller, *Religion,* pp. 111 ff., whose account is based on Heinrich Weinel, *Die deutsche evangelische Kirche* (Gotha, 1933).
70. Rosenberg, *Der Mythos des zwanzigsten Jahrhunderts.*
71. Cf. Keller, *Religion,* pp. 103 ff.
72. Bergmann, *Deutsche Nationalkirche,* cited by Keller, *Religion,* p. 108, n. 1.
73. "A Confession of Faith", cited by Keller, *Religion,* pp. 178 ff.
74. The Second Synod met at Berlin-Dahlem, October 18–20, 1934.
75. "The Theological Declaration of Barmen", *The Book of Confessions,* Second Edition (New York, 1970), Part II, par. 8.11.
76. *Ibid.,* par. 8.12.
77. *Ibid.,* par. 8.15.
78. *Ibid.,* par. 8.18.
79. *Ibid.,* par. 8.21.
80. *Ibid.,* par. 8.24.
81. *Ibid.,* par. 8.27.
82. Karl Barth, "Lutherfeier 1933", *Theologische Existenz Heute* (München, 1933), "Vorwort", p. 3.
83. *Ibid.,* p. 20.
84. Barth's dialectical period runs roughly from 1922, the date of the second edition of *The Epistle to the Romans,* to 1927, when he published his *Christliche Dogmatik.*
85. Emil Brunner, *Natur und Gnade, zum Gespräch mit Karl Barth* (Tübingen, 1934).

86. Karl Barth, *Nein! Antwort an Emil Brunner* (München, 1934). Both Brunner's *Natur und Gnade* and Barth's *Nein!* have been translated into English under the title *Natural Theology* by John Baillie (London, 1946).

87. Emil Brunner, *Natur und Gnade,* Second Edition (Tübingen, 1935) pp. I-VI.

88. *Ibid.,* p. VI.

89. Barth, "No!", *Natural Theology,* p. 122.

90. *Ibid.,* pp. 120 ff.

91. Brunner, "Nature and Grace", *Natural Theology,* p. 30.

92. *Ibid.,* p. 25.

93. *Ibid.*

94. *Ibid.,* p. 31. Italics added.

95. *Ibid.,* p. 32.

96. *Ibid.,* p. 55.

97. *Ibid.,* p. 56.

98. Cf. Howe, *Mensch und Physik,* p. 25, and Torrance *Theological Science,* pp. 63 ff.

99. Barth, "No!", *Natural Theology,* p. 100.

100. *Ibid.,* p. 101.

101. *Ibid.,* p. 111.

102. *Ibid.*

103. *Ibid.,* p. 123.

104. *Ibid.,* p. 126.

105. John Calvin, *Institutes of the Christian Religion, The Library of Christian Classics* XX, XXI, ed. John T. McNeill, 2 vols. (Philadelphia, 1960), Book I, Ch. V.11.

106. *Ibid.,* Book I, Ch. V.13.

107. Otto Weber, "Forward to the German Edition", *Karl Barth's Church Dogmatics* (London, 1953), p. 9.

108. Karl Barth, *Evangelical Theology, An Introduction* (New York, 1963).

109. Edmund Schlink, "Thesen über Theologie und Naturwissenschaften", *Evangelische Theologie,* 7. Jahrgang (München, 1947–48), p. 93. The tenor of Schlink's statements bears on the separation of theology and natural science.

110. Cf. Barth, *Church Dogmatics,* III/1, x.

111. Cf. Reginald Fuller, *The Foundations of New Testament Christology* (New York, 1965).

112. Cf. John McIntyre, "Models in Christology", *The Shape of Christology* (London, 1966), Section 3, pp. 55 ff.

113. Bernhard Bavink, *Das Christentum im Rahmen der Gegenwartskultur* (Bielefeld, 1957), p. 31 cited by Herbert Meschkowski, *Das Christentum im Jahrhundert der Naturwissenschaften* (München, 1961), p. 123. A "theologoumenon" is a private theological opinion over against recognized doctrine.

114. Bavink's position shows the extreme delicacy of moving theology away from scriptural concepts into motifs which are thought to be compatible with modern science.

115. Bavink, *Christentum,* pp. 121 ff.

116. Hence the Apostle Paul can say, "Even if we or an angel from heaven should preach to yŏu a gospel contrary to that which we preached to you, let him be accursed" (Gal. 1:8).

117. Barth, *Church Dogmatics* III/2, 10 f.

118. It will be remembered that even Schleiermacher warned against adopting philosophies which shut out the expression of faith. Cf. above, p. 85.

119. Barth, "The Preface to the First Edition", *Romans,* p. 1. Cf. "Vorwort zur ersten Auflage", *Römerbrief,* p. v. The passage, though written in Barth's first volume on theology, may still be recognized as indicating his *Magna Carta* with regard to the authority of the witness of Scripture.

120. Barth, *Romans,* p. 1; *Römerbrief,* p. v.

121. Reginald Fuller, *Introduction to the New Testament* (London, 1966); Oscar Cullmann, *Christologie des Neuen Testaments* (Tübingen, 1957); Thomas Weeden, *Traditions in Conflict* (Philadelphia, 1971); Helmut Koester and James Robinson, *Trajectories in the New Testament* (Philadelphia, 1971); *et al.*

122. Günter Howe, *Die Christenheit im Atomzeitalter* (Stuttgart, 1970), p. 23.

123. Hans Urs von Balthasar, *Karl Barth. Deutung und Darstellung seiner Theologie* (Köln, 1951), pp. 210 ff.

124. This trend is obvious in the works of Weizsäcker, Howe and Müller.

125. Latest estimates are that the sun is about 10-15 billion years old.

126. Bultmann's plea that the faith present the true *skandalon* (offense or stumbling block) rather than a false one has relevance at this point. Rudolf Bultmann, *Jesus Christ and Mythology* (New York, 1958), p. 36; cf. pp. 17 f. and Rudolf Bultmann, "New Testament and Mythology", *Kergyma and Myth* (London, 1954), p. 44. This does not mean, however, that we should necessarily accept Bultmann's existentialist interpretation of the gospel which is certainly as individualistically oriented and as subjectively pietistic as that of the History of Religions School which it is thought to replace. Cf. Bultmann, *Jesus Christ,* pp. 14 f. Bultmann's presupposition that "all our thinking today is irrevocably shaped by modern science", however, generally agrees with our thesis. *Ibid.,* p. 3; cf. *Ibid.,* p. 5n.

127. Bonhoeffer, *Letters and Papers,* p. 282. It is of more than little note that Bonhoeffer was thinking these thoughts at the same time he was reading Weizsäcker's *World View of Physics* in his prison cell in Berlin-Tegel. In it, Weizsäcker cites the phrase which we noted above from the French astronomer Laplace that has been famous in discussions of Bonhoeffer's thought. "Modern man needs no recourse to the 'working hypothesis' called 'God'". *Ibid.,* p. 325, cf. above p. 33.

128. *Ibid.,* pp. 325 ff. The early Christians, because they rejected the Hellenistic deities, were denounced as "atheists".

129. Daniel Lamont, *Christ and the World of Thought* (Edinburgh, 1934), p. 10.

130. From my notes taken from the lectures of Professor T. F. Torrance in Divinity, 1953–1954 during my first year as a student at the University of Edinburgh.

Chapter V

Crisis and Dialogue

Over three hundred years ago, Blaise Pascal, Christian philosopher and mathematician, viewed the world of his day with the same anxiety with which we at times are prone to view the world of our day. "We rush carelessly over the edge of the precipice after putting something in front of us to prevent our seeing it."[1] Our fate, as Pascal pointed out so poignantly, is determined not by our intention but by our blindness. In many instances we are unable to discern reality as it is because we have programmed ourselves to *focus out* what really exists. Consequently we discern partial reality at best, an illusory world at worst. It is not evil nor malevolence which is our greatest danger, but a lack of focus or a wrong focus which results largely both *from* and *in* wrong-headedness. The situation is such that our best intents may very well lead to the destruction of that which we wish to preserve.

Challenge and Response

The biologist Friedrich Oehlkers paints an enlightening if rather dark picture of the situation from the point of view of nature.

> For the animal and plant world, man is the very incarnation of evil itself. He is equipped with superior sinister powers. He goes around in all his ways according to his own caprice. He plants vegetation where and how he will and he destroys it again according to his pleasure. He modifies plant life according to his own shortsighted advantage because he possesses only a superficial knowledge of the laws of change and the vegetation follows him willing and still. The destruction, however, which man

causes to the planet that has been entrusted to him is so terrible
and at the same time so irreversible that in the long run in
destroying the planet he must also destroy himself.[2]

If, perhaps somewhat in contrast to Pascal's view, we in our
generation are becoming aware of the real dangers that we face
not only as individuals and nations but as humanity and indeed
as a whole planet, we would seem to have little reason at the
moment to be more optimistic than he was. The configurations
resulting from the political circumstances of the world divided
and enforcing that division through reciprocal threat of atomic
arsenals combined with the wanton exploitation of the planet's
raw materials and the ecological destruction present an awe-
some picture indeed. Our continued pollution of water,
atmosphere and land along with the energy crisis and our
inability to cope with the nuclear situation including the possibility of accidents, the actuality of powerful, poisonous atomic
wastes and the equally poisonous outworn atomic installations
in addition to population problems, all bode ominously for the
future. There is, of course, at least some sign of hope in the fact
that we are aware of our problems. At the same time our
awareness forces us to realize that as a whole humanity and the
planet on which our humanity depends may be sick if not
"terminally ill".

The German neurologist and philosopher Viktor von
Weizsäcker (1886–1957) has reminded us that "'to disease
belong not only angina, tuberculosis and cancer . . ., culture,
politics, art, science, and religion have diseases as well'".[3] With
regard to humanity the symptoms run the gamut from depres-
sive withdrawal from reality in an over-absorption in our work
and occupations to irrational attempts to flay the world in
terrorist activity. More acceptable and hence perhaps more
subtly dangerous is the concentration of serious effort toward
goals which are immediately achievable and individually
advantageous to the detriment of long-range accomplishments
with universal benefit. Eventually the process may end in the
"self-fulfilment" of certain individuals, groups and nations at
the expense of and through exploitation of others and the
planet as a whole.

The Heidelberg philosopher Georg Picht points to our situation with a poignant statement, "The scientist flees into his

speciality, politicians into the so-called 'realist politics', the dreamer flees into terrorist activity and the public consciousness in the consumer culture".[4] In his congratulatory address on behalf of C. F. von Weizsäcker on the occasion of Weizsäcker's receiving the Peace Prize from the German Booksellers Association in 1963, Picht goes on in the same vein:

> Weizsäcker has seen with inexorable clarity that a world catastrophe is inevitable when we, as in past history, allow ourselves to continue to be driven by the dynamic of the social processes in an incalculable power play. Humanity must put itself in the position whereby, according to the injunction of Genesis 1:26 it can take over responsibility for its history. It must shape what it has up to now only suffered to happen. This means, however, that rationality must permeate not only nature and not only, as in psychoanalysis, the unconscious levels of the soul, but penetrate our collective processes and modify them, for up to now it is out of these processes that most important historical upheavals have come. We need a therapy of the historical world. We need a therapy of society and the only medium for this therapy available to us is reason.[5]

In attempting to analyse the problems of our "sick-situation", or perhaps better to prescribe a goal toward which a rational therapy may be directed, the mathematician John von Neumann (1903–1957) coined the term *Überleben*. The term can perhaps best be translated simply as "survival". For Neumann *Überleben* in its full sense meant not only practical survival in physical terms but the maintenance and the continuation of that which makes life worth living. Survival thus moves beyond the maintenace of life and includes the attainment of "the good life". "The good life" refers to the enhancement of life not only for the select few, as has been the case until now, but for all, for all who live now *and* for all who live in the future. Thus the concept *Überleben* has immeasurable, almost boundless implications for the way we structure our existence, for the goals we set, for the way we use our raw materials, for the way we create and use energy, for the way we transport and house ourselves, grow and distribute our food and dispose of or recycle our waste, as well as the way we form ourselves in family, social and political units.

As to the future, the American theoretical physicist Freeman

J. Dyson and Professor Gerard O'Neill of Princeton University dream of cities in space. Over a decade ago, at the Conference of Physicists in Salzburg in 1969, Dyson argued for space habitation by saying, "Humanity needs an alternative possibility to this over-populated planet and therefore must be able to spread out into space".[6] Subsequently O'Neill has become an advocate of space communities, energy-gathering stations, factories and even farms.[7] Eventually the space cities may become a reality if indeed space existence is possible without too drastic a calcium loss in the body's skeletal structure, for instance, such as that recorded in the cases of both Soviet and American astronauts who have lived in space for up to three-month periods. However, chances are that the concentration of money, energy and material necessary for such efforts may well cause us to focus out our more immediate problems rather than focusing in on them. Even if the American space shuttle becomes a practical means of transportation to and from space stations, any appreciable extension of *Lebensraum* (space for living) won by sending people into space and having them occupy giant revolving space stations in orbit around the earth would be gained at a high price indeed. Were the number of space residents to reach into the millions and, given the fact as Adrian Berry has proposed that energy would be produced by the sun and raw materials taken from the moon, asteroids or perhaps even from cosmic dust,[8] eventually the psychological, social, political, economic and environmental problems that are bound to arise in artificial space cities will most likely be similar to those we already know on the natural spaceship, earth. At any rate spatial enterprises of this kind will not take place soon. Though one would rightly be accused of "Ludditism", if one were to advocate an end to space-exploration, it would seem that rather than an over-concentration on space habitation and alternative planets urgent concentration on the opportunities and problems of this one is called for.

We need a rationale for setting proper goals and motivation for adjusting our lives toward their achievement. In face of the optimism of Dyson, O'Neill and Berry, Picht no doubt sounds somewhat pessimistic when he says:

> The dream of the unlimited possibilities was a mad illusion. The technical world is a world of dreadful limited possibilities. The

hungry millions will not be able to migrate to another star. The resources on earth are not inexhaustible. The faster the expansion of science and technology is driven forward, the faster it reaches its non-transgressible limits.[9]

Picht is not nearly so pessimistic nor so rationalistically sadistic as the biologist Garret Hardin, who has coined the phrase "life-boat ethic". Hardin urges us not only to accept things as they are in the "overbirth", "underfed", "have not" nations of the world but to accept the fact that the less we do about the situation the better off we will be. Since those less provident and able tend to multiply at the expense of others who are more foresighted and talented, they threaten ruin to all of us.

> Every Indian life saved through medical or nutritional assistance from abroad diminishes the quality of life for those who remain, and subsequent generations.[10]

Hence Hardin advises us simply to write off the poor populations of India, Pakistan and Bangladesh. This "triage" policy[11] applied to nations rather than to the severely wounded by which, as sometimes happened in the Vietnam conflict, only those who were considered to have a chance of survival were given medical treatment, may seem rational but it also represents "closed-system thinking". In such a system, as in Newtonian science, the future is considered to be only an extension and extrapolation of the past. Such predictions, because they tend to stifle imagination and the search for unheard-of and undreamed-of solutions, then become self-fulfilling prophecies.

As over against Hardin's "life-boat ethics" which would discriminate against the present poor populations of the world, one might put the shoe on the other foot, as it were, and listen to E. F. Schumacher's judgement that it is the "advanced nations" of the world with their voracious appetites for energy which present the main problem for survival. Hence, Schumacher has stated that the world cannot afford the United States, Western Europe or Japan.[12]

Somewhat more balanced and certainly more pleasant, at least for those of us who are "privileged to live in the 'developed countries'", is Barry Commoner's analysis. According to Commoner, who is director of Washington University's Center for Biology of Natural Systems, "the amount of food crop produced in the world at present is sufficient to provide an adequate diet to about eight billion people—more than twice the world's population".[13]

Alan S. Miller, author of *The Population Bomb Explodes at Home,* emphasizes Commoner's thesis that poverty breeds over-population and thus that the population problem is essentially an economic one. He amplifies with the statement:

> Unfortunately most people still believe with Malthus and Hardin that the real problem can be blamed on the world's poor. We ignore the fact that Holland's population density is 960 per square mile—far higher than Asia's 200, Latin America's 36 or Africa's 30.[14]

Yet, while the population growth of Holland, like the rest of Western Europe, Japan, the United States and the Soviet Union, is 1% or less, that of the poor or "lesser developed countries" of Colombia, Bangladesh, Pakistan, the Philippines and Thailand had growth rates of over 3% in 1973. The thesis is that "people are not poor because they have large families, they have large families because they are poor". The statement of an Indian farmer serves to illustrate this point: "You think I am poor because I have too many children. If I didn't have my sons, I wouldn't have half the property I do. And God knows what would happen to me and their mother when we are too old to work and earn."[15]

Poverty conditions dictate that the average village peasant couple must bear 6.3 children to be 95% certain that *one* son will survive this father's 65th birthday.[16] China has brought down its birth rate from 2.6% before the revolution to 1.4% since 1974 simply by eliminating dire poverty and offering economic security. Hence "the Chinese have found a way to cut population growth at its roots".[17] The point is that our focus is determinative of our judgement and our judgement determinative of the course of action we decide on or do not decide upon. If we are to act humanely and embark on a course which is designed to approximate to Neumann's *Überleben,* then there must be elimination of poverty, redistribution of wealth, readjustments of the world's economic systems and greater distribution of justice at all levels. *Überleben* will have a chance of success, however, only by judicious use of the best science and technology available to us.

Thus there is no turning back the clock, no stopping the

earth to get off, no island of calm outside the chaotic situation in which we live and in which the scientific technological process takes place. In sum, if we wish to survive, there is no giving up science and technology. In the face of the rather popular but romantic idea that we would solve all problems by giving up our scientific and technological ways, escape from the world and its complications, and "go back to nature" where each of us would live beside his private "Walden Pond", as did Henry David Thoreau (1817–1862) in the middle of the nineteenth-century,[18] it may be necessary to remind ourselves not only that there are far too few ponds to go around, but that the only "nature" we know is that which we affect one way or another.

Rather than being something which is, nature is that which *is in development* and, as far as earth is concerned, we are the ones largely responsible for the development. Nature is thus a cooperative effort between humanity, the conscious part of nature, and the rest of nature as provided by the planet earth and the energy of the solar system. Nature, in respect to our world, is what *results* from the application of science and technology in, to, and with the environment of the planet, the solar system, the galaxy and eventually the cosmos.

Hence all that we see and know is continually subject to change. The process at one and the same time is extremely dangerous but may not be interrupted. Again, to quote Picht:

> Every stoppage would immediately destroy the whole system of science and technology. The ability out of which science and technology exist have, as it were, a special characteristic that they must atrophy when they cannot move out beyond themselves . . .[19]

The question is not whether we continue the development of science and technology. Rather the question is, "What direction should the development as a whole take?" Hence certain developments which may be seen as destructive of overall survival goals may have to be halted. These are well-known and run all the way from controlling pollution of air, water and land, the outlawing of the use of certain insecticides and chemicals, to policies concerning more exotic projects such as putting a moratorium on atmospheric testing of atomic devices, the shutting down of the American SST and the use of the utmost precaution in certain virus experimentations, even halting them at times until precautionary measures can insure reasonable safety. This includes re-examination of the need for nuclear power, and if it is needed, extreme caution in all further development.

An eloquent statement in this direction has been made by biologist Charles Birch:

> We have been warned as Noah was warned. Skeptics laughed and ridiculed then as they do now. Skeptics drowned and Noah, the original prophet of ecological doom, survived. We are warned that a flood of problems now threatens the existence of our industrial society. But this time the ark cannot be built of wood and caulking. Its foundation will be a new awareness of the meaning of life, of the life of all creatures both great and small. Its name will be the ecologically sustainable and socially just global society. If this ark cannot be made water-tight in time, industrial society will sink, dragging under prophets of doom as well as skeptics and critics.[20]

In a world of limited options, those which are judged beneficial must be promoted and those which are judged harmful or even doubtful must be halted. The decisions in this regard will not be easy ones. However, as in the realm of faith in which the Apostle Paul could advise his readers, "Test everything; hold fast what is good" (1 Thess. 5:21), so in the realm of life everything must continually be assessed and re-assessed in order that what is necessary for survival may be maintained and promoted and what is destructive be given up. Survival will result from a reaffirmation and a redefinition of goals and from a reformation of the practices which, *according to the best judgement available,* will lead to the fulfilment of these goals.[21]

Our survival demands, therefore, at least something of a reorientation in which our limits are considered to be not hindrances to but opportunities toward the achievement of the "good life". Rather than the end of the dream, survival calls for a broader, deeper, more universal and hence more realistic dream. It calls for a new rationality, an opening up of conceptuality to include goals and the means toward their achievement. It calls for our seeing the world as integral to the maintenance and development of our personal lives and the lives of all contemporary peoples as well as those of future generations.

The demand for "survival", defined, following Neumann, as survival *for all* as the achievement of the "good life" *for all,* has, of course, immediate practical application to our world. Minimal demands of the programme for survival include at least maintenance of world peace, the banning of world hunger and the spread of health, education, welfare and just economic opportunity for all the world's peoples. Faith enters the picture both in universalizing our view, "The earth is the Lord's and the fullness thereof, the world and those who dwell therein" (Ps. 24:1), and in providing the impetus to carry out the demands of a reoriented life — all creatures are God's creation. To love God is to love all people and all creation. *The demands will become real to us only when and to the degree we believe them necessary.* It is only when, deep down within our souls. we become convinced of the necessity for change, when the goals of a new humanity and a new earth glow before us in inflamed imagination that we will be enabled to conceive the quality of life which is consistent with faith and made possible through science and technology.

Hence our theological concepts which include our ethical perspectives must be spelled out, reconsidered and expanded to include the assessments of the powers of the scientific technological world by which means the goals conceived may be achieved. Georg Picht, in his congratulatory address to Weizsäcker cited above, calls for "a faith-enlightened reason" as necessary in reconsidering the demands of our dominating the earth according to Genesis 1:26. "In this way", as Picht puts it, "Weizsäcker makes his transition to theology". Picht also points out, however, that Weizsäcker "acknowledges that the theology which he finds necessary does not at present exist".[22] As today our theology seems inadequate to take the world seriously, so also our science seems incapable of a conceptuality that is both universal and purposeful. An intensive open dialogue between theology and natural science could possibly result in greater conceptual adequacy for both.

Göttingen Conversations

Perhaps the most outstanding example of an attempt at an intensive and enduring dialogue between natural science and theology is that which took place annually in Göttingen between the years 1948 and 1959. The beginning of the "Göttingen Conversations" between physicists and theologians goes back to a conversation between the mathematician Günter Howe and the physicist Carl Friedrich von Weizsäcker on a train between Marburg and Göttingen. The two Göttingen professors were returning from a conference in Marburg in January 1938 just a few months before Otto Hahn (1879–1968) and Fritz Strassmann (1902–   ) discovered atomic fission in their laboratory at the University of Berlin.

The mention of Hahn and Strassmann's discovery is important in this context because it was in the heat of the questions that arose in 1948 regarding the use and control of atomic devices three years after the close of World War II, that Howe took practical steps to set up the first of the conversations which he and Weizsäcker had talked about ten years before. Howe traced the heritage of the inspiration for the necessity of conversations between theology and natural science to the lecture entitled *Religion und Naturwissenschaft* ("Religion and Natural Science") delivered in 1937 by the physicist and dedicated churchman Max Planck, the author of Quantum Theory.[23] Planck's lecture, made in the midst of the Church's struggle against Nazism, expressed his conviction as to the interdependence of natural science and faith. The implicit but real point of the lecture, delivered four years after the Nazi take-over, was to reject the Nazis' double-barrelled attempt to discredit faith, on the one hand, and to prescribe a science in line with nationalistic interests, on the other. Hence Planck gave a subtle but definite affirmative answer to the question as to whether or not one educated in the natural sciences could at the same time be a person of genuine faith.

> Religion and Natural Science do not exclude one another as many today believe or fear. Rather do they complement and condition one another. Certainly the most direct evidence for the compatibility of religion and natural science is the historical fact that it was primarily the greatest natural scientists of all time, men such as Kepler, Newton, Leibniz, in particular, who were deeply religious . . . Together religion and natural science lead the constant, continual, never flagging struggle against scepticism and dogmatism, against unfaith and superstition.

The word that sets us free in this struggle, the word which has been expressed from time immemorial and bears upon all the future, is *Onward toward God*.[24]

The fact that Planck had not freed himself altogether from the closed-system thinking of the Newtonian world-view is evident from his exclusion of "miracle",[25] and his constant tendency to place natural science in the realm of *knowledge* and belief in God in the realm of *faith*. That is to say, he held that science functions primarily through *understanding* while religion for the most part utilizes sentiment *(Gesinnung)*.[26] Planck's comparison of God with natural lawfulness, and inheritance of Newtonian conceptuality, was not particularly fortunate either.[27] Nevertheless, as Howe was to emphasize again and again, Planck's conviction that natural science and religion without any doubt agree with rather than contradict one another[28] was of decisive import at the time and continues to be decisive for our time.

Planck's thoughts stayed with Howe. Following the plan which he and Weizsäcker had discussed some ten years previously, in 1938, Howe called together about twenty-five natural scientists, philosophers and theologians in Göttingen to talk with one another about the mutual responsibility of science, on the one hand, and theology, on the other. After the first meeting the conversations between physicists and theologians continued to be held under Howe's initiative at Göttingen for eleven consecutive years.[29]

Howe conceived the task of the physicist-theologian circle as a continuation of the struggle of the Confessing Church which had attempted to relate faith to the whole of life.[30] He was convinced that discussions of this kind would show that theology and natural science would find a way of being of service to one another. The Confessing Church, during the Nazi period, had shown the political and social relevance of the faith by resisting the Nazi attempts to manipulate it and its message. It had brought to life the extra-ecclesiastical dimension of the Gospel. This legacy, Howe hoped, would inspire theologians who had been active in the Confessing Church movement to direct their energies in shaping the post-war world. It was the world of the atomic age which, whether we like it or not, physics and technology had created. And whether we like it or not, the world of the atomic age is the only world available. As Howe saw it, it was a world which posed ultimate questions in a practical and ominous way, questions which were on the same level of gravity as those once posed by Nazism, questions which must, therefore, concern the theologians as well as the scientists.

Because the nuclear age had demonstrated that the very texture of life and the life of the planet, for better or worse, was at the mercy of science and technology, Howe was convinced that the time (1948) was ripe for a re-orientation of theology toward natural science in general and physics in particular. He was, however, under no illusion that theology and physics could or should be synthesized. Since that winter (February 14, 1931) when Howe had been "converted to theology" by Barth's Hamburg lecture *Die Not der Evangelischen Kirche* ("The Peril of the Protestant Church"), he had remained an energetic student of Barth. Faithful to his mentor, he explained the importance of theology in relation to the other sciences by summarizing Barth's argument to this effect.

> Theology is in no way a part of an ordered cosmos but a stop-gap in an unordered one. It could well be that all of the sciences working together in the sphere of the Church, would render a special theology superfluous. Theology does not have at its disposal a special basis for knowledge which might straight away become actual in every other science, nor is it aware of an area of reality which is necessarily hidden from any science whatsoever. Secular science really need not be "secular", need not be "heathen". Whoever contests this in principle combines a despair of the world with an over-evaluation of the "Christian world in a way which is compatible neither with Christian hope nor with Christian humility. Theology as a special science is only to be justified as a relative and practical necessity. All sciences at their highest point could be theology. The fact that they are not does not call for complaint or for justification here.[31]

Howe then goes on to explain Barth's position:

> In line with this understanding derived from Karl Barth, theology has again placed itself over against the other sciences. In contrast to the synthesis-happy theology of the previous century which managed to earn little respect from these other sciences, a theology which follows its own course unperturbed about such matters as an inherent point of contact with God

(Anknüpfungspunkt), a vestigal image of God in humankind unaffected by the Fall *(Imago Reste),* etc., will again become a relevant matter for philosophers, historians, physicists, etc. It will become this without making any attempt, even as a venture, to carry on a conversation with the partner outside the walls of the Church and thereby place itself in a position of unfaith. Through its own particular service theology opens up the only possible avenue for a point of contact between God and man, that point of contact which God alone can create.[32]

By the time Howe called the physicists and theologians together, however, he had become uneasy with Barth's dichotomy between theology and natural science. He felt that the dichotomy posed the danger of carrying Barth to the point where, for all intents and purposes, he would ignore any real relevance of science for theology. To reiterate, Howe remained convinced that the Barmen Declaration, that *Magna Carta* of the Confessing Church for which Barth had been chiefly responsible, had been of inestimable value in preventing at least a part of the German Church from succumbing to Nazism. This same concern, therefore, must again prove itself in the post-war world, this time in conversation with natural science.[33] The Church had gained a new consciousness in its struggles against Nazism, a consciousness which resulted in the re-establishment of its foundations upon the Word of God alone.

Howe was well aware of the fact that in the early thirties this new mentality, as he called it, had enabled Barth's theology to gain a clear victory over natural theology. Fourteen years later, however, he felt that the time had come for this fundamental realization to be carried forward and expanded with relevance to the changed conditions of the post-war period. It was time for comprehensive collaboration with the natural sciences which, through technology, had the world in its grasp. To Howe's mind, therefore, the Göttingen conversations between theologians and physicists were to be the beginning of a whole new point of departure for theological thinking.[34]

For Howe it was of the greatest importance that Barth's theology, according to his own assessment, provided an entry into conversation with post-Newtonian physics at two points. The first was the parallel which Howe found between the double nature of reality as enunciated in Niels Bohr's

Copenhagen interpretation of the theory of complementarity and the emphasis on love and justice in Barth's doctrine of God. The second was the coincidence between Barth's explanation of time as belonging to finite creation and Einstein's concept of the finite universe. Hence, when he had organized the first of the Göttingen conversations, Howe wrote to Barth with expectation and hope:

> The theologians have had 25 years to occupy themselves with your thoughts. If that had taken place with only a little more intensity then the situation in the Church would look different from what it is. Then there would be at least one theology which would be able adequately to portray what you have said about the subject of time and could carry on a conversation with Heisenberg in your name. . . .The physicists have earned the right that you should have a little time for them.[35]

The conversations in Göttingen took place annually for twelve consecutive years. The fact that their results never matched Howe's initial anticipation was foreshadowed by the answers he received to his first invitations. Karl Barth, Howe's "theological father", close correspondent, and to Howe's mind the leading theologian of the day, could not accept the first invitation because of prior engagements. In spite of Howe's friendship and urgent letters Barth refused invitations to the subsequent meetings as well.[36] Unfortunately Professor Karl Heim, the only theologian of note at the time who considered the liaison between theology and natural science of prime importance, was hindered by ill health from attending the conversations also.

Hence, while physicists of the calibre of C. F. von Weizsäcker, Werner Heisenberg and Pascual Jordan (1902–   ) were open and available for the conversations, to Howe's astonishment the theologians upon whom he had counted most, Karl Barth and his followers, were extremely reluctant to venture into foreign territory. The irony of the matter was that those who understood and followed Barth on the theological faculty at Göttingen and who took part in the conversations — Otto Weber and Ernst Wolf — were not able to prevent their colleague, Friedrich Gogarten, from becoming the actual "conversation partner of the physicists".[37] Gogarten's affinities for a "natural theology" manifested themselves in his earlier collaboration with the German Christian movement against which the Confessing Church, which had given Howe the inspiration for calling the conversations in the first place, was established.

In the early twenties Barth and Gogarten had been associates. Both had been influenced by the writing of Kierkegaard, saw eye to eye regarding the bankruptcy of nineteenth-century liberal theology and in the early twenties joined in a common effort to reform the Church. However, so decisive were Gogarten's "traitorous tendencies" in espousing for a time the German Christian cause and joining a movement sympathetic to the Nazis in 1934, that Barth and Gogarten saw one another but once afterwards. The occasion was in Göttingen where Barth was invited to a lecture after the war. They recognized one another's presence but Barth was so hurt by what he considered to be Gogarten's betrayal that he thought it best not to try to speak to his former friend.[38] Howe could not have been ignorant of the impasse between Barth and Gogarten. Nor does he hide the fact that he considered Gogarten's theology, in spite of its intellectual powers, *passé*. Nevertheless he wrote to Barth telling him that he was grateful to Gogarten for doing the physicists the favour of being open to their questions while he (Barth) was not.

The fact that such conversations were in fact "foreign territory" for both the theologians and the physicists who attended no doubt explains why the members who took part in the first consultation were in general somewhat ill at ease. The theologians seemed hesitant about taking scientific categories seriously. According to Howe, the physicists too were somewhat reluctant to accept theological implications for their science.[39] Weizsäcker put the matter plainly, "They wanted to go only so far into the Church as they could take the whole of their physics with them".[40] Nevertheless Howe remained hopeful. A year after the first conversation he again admonished his friend Barth. "The point will soon be reached where it will not only be of importance that the physicists make contact with theology but where the particular theological standpoint at which the meeting with the physicists will take place will be significant."[41]

Howe's hopes, however, proved to be in vain, for Barth

never joined the conversations. Neither was the theological point ever reached at which the proposal for a new theology in relation to the realities of natural science could be put forward.[42]

Continuing Dialogue

In spite of disappointment Howe's impetus was not lost altogether. In 1951 the Dutch Study Commission "Faith and Natural Science" was founded after the Göttingen pattern. The Dutch group, inaugurated by Dr C. F. Dippel in Eindhoven, took part in the Göttingen conversations on a number of occasions with practically all their members present. Interest widened, so that at the end of May 1958 the Göttingen circle along with the Dutch Study Commission met with a number of groups from England, France and Switzerland and a larger number of individual representatives from other countries at the Ecumenical Institute at Bossey, Switzerland, for the first dialogue between theology and natural science on a broad ecumenical basis. The Bossey meeting aroused the interest of the Commission of the Churches for International Affairs of the World Council of Churches and in August 1958, the Executive Committee of that Commission, meeting at Nyborg, Denmark, made the pronouncement:

> In particular we need a theological interpretation of the new nature of the atomic age and the terrible dilemma between the demands which preserve life and maintain justice and those which order exploration. We need an interpretation guided by Christian faith in revelation.

The result was that four years later in October 1962, the Conference of European Churches met at Nyborg under the theme "The Church in Europe and the Crisis of Modern Man". Howe, himself, delivered the primary address entitled "Man's Scientific Attitude to the Universe and its Challenge to Theology", using the occasion to present his programme for theology and natural science.

The gist of Howe's statement was as follows: We find ourselves in the midst of a second phase of the second technical revolution which humankind has known. The first was the neolithic revolution which transformed humans from hunters and food gatherers to tillers of soil and cattle raisers. The second revolution, the scientific-technical revolution, began just two hundred years ago in 1776 when James Watt produced the first useful industrial steam engine. At present we are entering the second phase of the scientific-industrial revolution, the atomic age. Humankind's technical development was marked by the use of wind, animal and water power. This technology, inherited from the ancient world, was enabled to grow into its modern, scientific-technological phase in the "Christian world" just because the Christian faith and its attendant theology had tamed creation so that the investigation and manipulation of creation became possible.

Progress has not been made on all fronts, however. The fateful outlook in medieval thought which divided reality into the spiritual and the material realms has continued to plague even "Christianized" western thought down to the present. The division which was systematized in the subject-object dichotomy of Descartes led to two fateful bifurcations. The first was the separation of the self from the world. The second was the separation of God from outward reality confining him to relations with the inward self. Thus Cartesian dualism, which continues its influences within both theology and natural science alike, is responsible also for the divorce between faith and natural science.

In the light of this state of affairs, Howe's plea was twofold. With regard to the Cartesian bifurcation of reality he argued that modern physics itself, particularly that of Heisenberg and Bohr, showed the way by which Descartes' dualism might be overcome. He insisted also, however, that while humankind must recognize the dominant position of science in the world today, acknowledge its determining contribution to humanity, and continue to utilize it for survival, we must take every precaution not to become subjugated to it.

It is imperative, Howe insisted, that we think out theology anew in the light of science. As mentioned above, he had already discerned the beginnings of this renewal of theology in Barth's doctrine of God where both justice and love are emphasized. For Howe this was analogous to Bohr's concept of complementarity wherein observations which are logically mutually exclusive are found to be mutually necessary.

Further, since in Heisenberg and Bohr the dimension of the historical was recognized to be integral to scientific observation and theory, modern physics seemed to imply a new logic for thought in general. By implication this logic ought to lead to a breakdown of the dichotomies that have arisen between the spiritual and the material, the self and the world, natural science and faith.[43] The wholistic view of reality which should result from such a conceptual outlook ought to have two direct implications. The first would be an integration of science and technology within a unified concept of reality. The new perspective should enable humankind to use the ever increasing power of the modern technological machine constructively rather than destructively as we often fear will be the case. Second, such thinking would also bring a new perspective to faith itself which might enable its liberating power to take hold of the practical aspects of life.

> It is only through a fresh experience of the freedom of God which governs history that Christianity can obtain the strength to play its part in liberating the material world and hence in liberating man.[44]

Howe died on July 28, 1968, a few weeks before his sixtieth birthday, too early to see his effort bear much fruit. The impetus of his work lives on, however. There is the *Evangelische Studiengemeinschaft* (The Protestant Study Fellowship) at Heidelberg which is supported by all of the Protestant Provincial Churches of Germany. The fellowship has both full-time staff and active members on call: natural scientists, theologians and philosophers throughout Germany whom the fellowship gathers together to consider and discuss pertinent scientific and technological problems which are of concern to the Church and the world. A whole range of concerns: the atomic threat, nuclear power, the population explosion and the third world, educational reform, ecological questions and the problem of survival, have been considered and publications resulting from these consultations have appeared. A second and related effort is to be found in the Max Planck Institute at Starnberger See south of Munich in which C. F. von Weizsäcker has, until recently, been leading a study entitled *Die Lebensbedingungen in dem wissenschaftlich-technischen Zeitalter* ("The Necessary Conditions for Life in the Scientific Technological Age"). A third result of Howe's impetus and perhaps the one that to date may have the most far-reaching consequence (an expanded successor of the European Council of Churches Conference held in 1962 under the title "The Church in Europe and the Crisis of Modern Man" referred to above) was the conference sponsored by the World Council of Churches on "Faith, Science, and the Future" at the Massachusetts Institute of Technology in July 1979. Delegates and accredited visitors from the world over met to hear addresses and join in seminars and deliberative sessions dealing with topics which ranged from the nature of science and faith, through science and education, theological and ethical issues in the manipulation of life, to questions bearing on the environment, population, nuclear weapons, energy, economics, justice and new advances in the biological and medical sciences. It is hoped that the conference report will be taken seriously by the world's ecclesiastical, scientific, economic and political communities is planning for the future.[45]

Following the recommendation of Section I of the conference, "The Nature of Science and the Nature of Faith", that smaller more specialized conferences should follow in the future, the Free University in Amsterdam called a conference under the theme "Concern About Science", on October 13-17, 1980. The conference committee was chaired by astronomer H. Verheul, a member of Group I at the Massachusetts Institute of Technology mentioned above. A more modest but directly related effort is the Task Team for the Dialogue Between Theology and Science under the auspices of the Council of Theology and Culture of the Presbyterian Church in the United States.

Another continuing effort in this direction is the establishment of the *Karl Heim Gesellschaft* or *Karl Heim Society*. The founding of this society in the name of the one theologian whose interest in science made him to be considered an outsider in his own time, indicates that the climate may be changing. Heim's three volumes on theology and natural science can now be considered classics in the field. The society, founded to support a biblical-Christian orientation in the scientific-technical world, has three goals:

1. Reprinting of the most important writings of Karl Heim,

2. Continuing the scientifically oriented inter-disciplinary confrontation, particularly as exercised by Heim and as applicable to new problem complexes, and

3. Making available pertinent literature, supplying lecturers, calling problem-oriented conferences and being responsible for meetings in local church congregations.[46]

Other groups who have interfaced faith and natural science and in some cases continue to do so are *Convivium* in Great Britain and *The Polanyi Society* in America, both of which are inspired by the inter-disciplinary thought of Michael Polanyi (1891–1976). For a number of years a group led by Donald Schriver, now president of Union Theological Seminary, New York, met in the interest of science and religion in the "Research Triangle" centered at Duke University. A group consisting, among others, of Charles West of Princeton Theological Seminary (who was a director of the Ecumenical Institute at the Howe-inspired meeting in 1958), Ian S. Barbour, Daniel Day Williams, William G. Pollard, Roger Shinn and Harold Schilling met as the Science and Theology Discussion Group concerned with the themes raised by Barbour's *Issues in Science and Religion* and Schilling's *The New Consciousness in Science and Religion*.[47] The Institute on Religion in the Age of Science centered in Chicago is closely connected with the periodical *Zygon, Journal of Religion and Science,* encourages the faith-science dialogue, and sponsors conferences which deal with specific themes in the general area of science and religion. Of far-reaching importance for the future of theology is the *Center of Theological Inquiry* established in Princeton, New Jersey, in 1979 and directed by Dr James I. McCord of Princeton Theological Seminary, New Jersey. The center is designed to encourage and support advanced research in the relations between theology and science.[48]

Thus, in some ways at least, we find ourselves in a continuing development of the happy situation referred to by Howe wherein the question, "Is the Christian faith important for the scientific research of the scientist and, if so, according to what perspective and within which parameters?"[49] is now being asked and seriously considered. It is a question which, according to Howe, would have been beyond conception in the age of the Enlightenment, amid the nineteenth-century liberalism, or even in the hey-day of the biblical theological movement. The question, however, is now being considered by numbers of qualified natural scientists and theologians alike. Thus there are at least some indications that we may be at the beginning of a development which will reverse much of the closed outlook of the last century.

There would seem to be little doubt about the fact that in the middle of the nineteenth-century natural science and especially physics, in questioning and to a certain extent attacking the then accepted concepts of faith, was one of the main forces driving scientists out of the Church and relegating theology to the antique shop. According to the German existentialist philosopher Martin Heidegger (1889–1976), physics of all the modern sciences both exhibits and conduces to the modern habit of mind which conceives of and determines reality according to the autonomous human reason.[50] As we have seen, nineteenth-century natural science considered humankind and nature as self-dependent, independent realities.[51] In its most advanced stages this development of Newtonian science as "perfected" by Laplace regarded the world including humankind as a rigid mechanistic system obeying inexorable and pre-established "laws", laws which became more and more evident as scientific procedures became more and more precise. God, if thought of at all, was considered superfluous as far as the world described by science was concerned. Hence according to the words of David Friedrich Strauss reflecting on the scientific mind of the mid-nineteenth-century, God was both "homeless" and "unemployed".[52]

In contrast we find today, in some instances at least, theologians taking natural science seriously and natural scientists taking theology seriously. Although it may well be true, as the mathematician Herbert Meschkowski has pointed out, that few of the natural scientists who take faith seriously are willing to accept the tenets of their Church's "orthodoxy" as such,[53] nevertheless, the conversation between theologians and

172 THEOLOGY AND SCIENCE IN MUTUAL MODIFICATION

natural scientists has developed and continues at a serious level. A growing number of writings touching upon and pertinent to both natural science and theology is evident as is the growing number of study groups and conferences where natural scientists and theologians consider the problems of humanity to be common problems, problems to which theology and natural science may together contribute helpful insight. The more intensively these discussions take place, the more ordinary this working together becomes, the sooner we may expect beneficial results.

Considering the fact that we are now once again beginning to regard theology as a science and theologians as scientists, it may not be out of place to look upon conversations between natural scientists and theologians in the terms with which Peter Medawar explained the kind of cooperation which took place between Jim Watson and Francis Crick in their discovery of DNA:

> In no other form of serious creative activity is there anything equivalent to a collaboration between scientists, which is a subtle and complex business, and a triumph when it comes off, because the skill and performance of a team of equals can be more than the sum of individual capabilities.[54]

Future Connotations

The future of serious collaboration between theologians and scientists may be regarded as hopeful largely because it is now apparent on all sides that the science which in the nineteenth-century drove the intellectuals out of the Church has changed.[55] Through the work of Faraday, Clerk Maxwell, Planck, Einstein, Jeans, Eddington, Heisenberg and Bohr, to name but a few, it has moved far beyond the nineteenth-century concept of a closed mechanistic universe and a deterministic view of reality. We are again beginning to realize, as Torrance emphasizes in the "General Foreword" to this series, that the phenomenal aspects of nature "point infinitely beyond themselves". Yet this "infinite beyond" impinges directly on all aspects of space-time calling on us to open our minds to the interimpinging realities of nature which are not at all obvious at the phenomenological level defined by space and time.

Thus in contrast to the Cartesian and Kantian dualism referred to above, Weizsäcker sees not only matter and energy as being ultimately one, he proposes that ultimately matter and mind are integral to and impinge upon one another.[56] Torrance's optimistic view-point is reflected in his statement:

> For the first time, then, in the history of thought, Christian theology finds itself in the throes of a new scientific culture which is not antithetical to it, but which operates with a non-dualistic outlook upon the universe which is not inconsistent with the Christian faith . . .[57]

Hence, though we would hardly want to adopt a view of nature as capable of revealing God, while rejecting another view of nature as incapable of mediating knowledge of him, we may well have to develop theological conceptualities which, to take a cue from Dietrich Bonhoeffer, enable us to express recognition of the fact that "God is transcendent in the midst of our life".[58] It was in this direction that Howe was evidently pointing when he wrote:

> God reveals himself in that he objectifies himself in a piece of the world's reality. Theology, therefore, has no other choice but to explicate this piece of historical-social (and also physical) reality with the materials of thought that are available at the time and thus to make them a part of the Church's proclamation and doctrinal system.[59]

In support, Howe quoted Ulrich Scheuner, a lawyer concerned with the "atom-question", "We will be able to solve the atom-question only when we meet the God-question in all its profundity".[60] Günter Howe, natural scientist that he was, was perhaps even more acute when he said, "Whereas classical physics [the Newtonian system] had a pronounced affinity to nineteenth-century liberal theology, the physicist of today expects of theology that it will think consistently from the point of view of miracle *(von Wunder her consequent denkt)*".[61]

Thus if we let our inspired imaginations move toward the horizon of hope, we may perhaps even dare to ask with Howe in words he cited from Heidegger:

> Are we indeed standing on the eve of the most enormous change of the whole earth and of the time of the historical realm in which it is suspended? Are we standing before the evening of a night leading to another kind of morning?[62]

We may dare to hope so. We may hope so, however, not because "God is in his heaven and all is right with the world", as Leibniz once said to substantiate his optimistic but somewhat naïve doctrine of pre-established harmony. Rather from the point of view of the Judaeo-Christian faith, this hope for "another kind of morning" is based on the ever-widening realization that science and technology, which developed in the West in the cradle of "Christian culture", are the proper expressions of faith in relation to nature. They are, as Professor of Old Testament Klaus Koch has said, "a proper extrapolation" of the Genesis command to be "fruitful and multiply, fill the earth and subdue it".[63]

Thus though it is sadly true, as Lynn White has pointed out, that western society has often used science and technology to exploit the environment, his contention that the imperative of the Genesis command has resulted in an "orthodox Christian arrogance toward nature" represents a misunderstanding.[64] Rather as Heidegger has put it, the exploitation of nature is a result of a "false objectification" of nature, a separating of nature from humankind so that humankind is "no longer the gardener of nature but nature's lord and possessor".[65] J. Robert Nelson's answer in this regard is simple and succinct. Exploitation is due not to the Genesis command but to sin and selfishness![66] The intent of Genesis, as Old Testament scholars Claus Westermann and Norbert Lohfink insist, is that humankind is to be responsible for nature, to care for it as a shepherd cares for his flock and to live in inner harmony with it.[67]

As God is the Lord of all creation including humankind, so humankind is created in his *image* to exercise a derivative dominion over creation. Adam and Eve were nature's "gardeners". They were to cultivate it, care for it and keep it in order. As they cared for nature, nature in turn was to provide for them. In that science and technology arose as a direct result of humankind's interaction with nature, Klaus Koch would seem to be quite correct in saying: "In Genesis 1, the whole programme of natural science and technology lies *in nuce* before us".[68]

In the New Testament the lordship of God over creation is exercised by Christ who is Lord of all. He is the "Almighty", the *pantocrator* (2 Cor. 6:18). It is confidence in that Lordship in the present that gives us the assurance that the *world* is to be saved (John 3:17), that the new heaven and the new earth will eventually become reality (Rev. 21:1) and that there are those who are called to become ministers and workers in the salvific process (2 Cor. 5:18–6:1). In the light of the eschatological promise of the salvation of the totality of reality, we may begin to understand, as the Apostle Paul put it (Rom. 8:18-25) that the whole of creation groans "in eager expectation as it waits for the revealing of the sons of God". Creation groans and we groan with it. Creation groans because it is subject to decay. We groan because although in solidarity with creation we suffer decay, we also know something of the glory of redemption which in the fullest sense includes the whole of creation.

It is the contrast between our broken distorted situation and our vision of wholeness, of reconciled reality, which causes our agony. At the same time, this vision of wholeness, which to some degree at least may be reflected in our actual situation, is the basis for hope. In this hope, a hope of salvation that has cosmic dimensions, we are quite literally saved by faith understood as "the assurance of things to come" (Heb. 11:1). Faith, then, affords us the kind of focus upon reality which inspires our minds to unify the totality of reality, insofar as we can penetrate into it, so that it becomes an inter-relational and inter-dependent whole which is caught up in the promise of eschatological fulfilment.

Modern science as well as modern theology are one in stressing that our ability to apprehend the universe is directly dependent upon the presuppositions which we bring to the attempt of understanding. Hence, we are beginning to see that, not only is faith built on a confessional basis, but science is basically confessional as well. Within the parameters of possibility, the reality we find is the reality we search for. The kind of a world we can soberly believe to exist is the kind of a world we can assist in bringing about. Solutions, therefore, wait both upon the imagination and the will to work toward necessary changes in the thought structures related to science and theology as well as reassessment of the way science and technology are employed.

Though the ecumenical conference at the Massachusetts Institute of Technology, "Faith, Science and the Future", and the one at the Free University in Amsterdam, "Concern About Science", mentioned above, were for the most part ethically oriented — hence they were concerned more with the applied science and the justification of its use rather than with the structures of science and their possible inter-relation with theological concepts of thought — there were attempts to discuss these inter-relationships at a basic level. At M.I.T. the addresses of both Robert Hanbury Brown and Gerhard Liedke, as well as the report of Section I, indicate a real effort to move into the kind of basic epistemological questions with which discussions between science and theology began at Göttingen with Günter Howe, C. F. von Weizsäcker, Pascual Jordan, Werner Heisenberg and others some thirty years ago.[69] One paragraph of the report of Section I is specific in this regard:

Faith and Science Complement and Penetrate Each Other
Since science cannot finally prove its concepts, it is also basically a confessional enterprise, characterized by "faith" in the intelligibility of nature, in the orderliness of the universe, etc. At the same time, it is an intellectual discipline which is subservient to its object and can therefore be defined only in relationship to that object. In that sense theology can also be called a "science". In any form of understanding, therefore, there is a faith factor and a science factor which complement one another.[70]

As God's partners in the salvation of the world our task has just begun. It is a task which will be dependent upon both theological and scientific thought for its basic conceptuality. It will make full use of science and technology both to *understand* the world in which we live and upon which we are dependent for life, and to *transmute* this thought into practicality. This does not mean that we necessarily accept the solutions which heretofore have grown out of science and technology (or those that have grown out of theology, for that matter) as the only possible ones or as adequate ones. Rather, if we are convinced that God is the Creator, Sustainer and Saviour of the entire world and of the whole of history, then it would seem rather mandatory that we make an effort to plan and work for a world in which history may be prolonged and survival, *Überleben,* becomes possible.

We of course "see in a glass darkly", as the Apostle Paul put it (1 Cor. 13:12), but we do see. That is the basis of our hope. The ability to see, however, also makes us responsible in the use of our sight and insight. Our vision will be justified in proportion to the universality of its scope. The validity of our perspective will be measured in terms of the way it encompasses human welfare, the welfare of the planet and eventually in terms of the welfare of the cosmos. The vision of what is possible becomes practical as our faith-informed focus moves by way of science and technology into a rationality that informs us of a new reality which is yet to be attained.

With this kind of vision we may be drawn into a future world, a world which we do not as yet know but which may well reveal itself to us as we approach it and engage ourselves in the struggle with it to bring it into being. This possibility lies beyond us to be sure. It may become a probability, however, because the same God who created the world out of nothing calls us to struggle on behalf of its re-creation.

Footnotes to Chapter V

1. Blaise Pascal, *Pensées*, trans. Martin Turnell (London, 1962), No. 183 (Louis Lafuma order), p. 200.

2. Friedrich Oehlkers, "Aus einer Rede, die der Biologe Friedrich Oehlkers 1957 auf dem Freiburger Universitäts-Jubiläum gehalten hat", cited by Müller, *Präparierte Zeit*, p. 499.

3. Victor von Weizsäcker, *Pathosophie* (Göttingen, 1956), p. 238 cited by Müller, *Präparierte Zeit*, p. 64.

4. Georg Picht, *Mut zur Utopie: Die grossen Zukunftsaufgaben* (München, 1969) cited by Müller, *Präparierte Zeit*, p. 122.

5. Georg Picht, *Bedingungen des Friedens* (Göttingen, 1964), pp. 35 f.

6. Freeman J. Dyson, "Menschheit und Weltall" (Festvortrag auf der 34. Physikertagung 1969 in Salzburg), *Physikalische Blätter*, 25. Jg. Heft 1 (1970), 7 ff. cited by Müller, *Präparierte Zeit*, p. 66.

7. Gerard O'Neill, *The High Frontier* (New York, 1978).

8. Adrian Berry projects such a possibility in his somewhat fantastic but none the less interesting book, *The Iron Sun* (Anderson, Ind., 1978), by the twenty-third century, cf. pp. 89 ff.

9. Georg Picht, *Prognose, Utopie, Planung* (Stuttgart, 1971), p. 40.

10. Garret Hardin, "The Case against Helping the Poor", *Psychology Today* (Sept. 1974), p. 124.

11. The term "triage" became the designation of the practice applied in situations where medical facilities were overwhelmed with numbers of wounded. The wounded were divided into three groups, hence the term "triage". In the first group were those judged to have little or no chance of survival no matter what treatment was given them. These were left to die. In the second group were those who were less severely wounded and who, it was decided, would respond if medical treatment was given immediately. These were treated as soon as possible. The least severely wounded who, it was thought, could survive at least for the time being, were placed in the third group. They were treated as time and the availability of facilities allowed.

12. Schumacher is quoted by J. Robert Nelson, *Science and Our Troubled Conscience* (Philadelphia, 1980), p. 157.

13. Barry Commoner, "How Poverty Breeds Overpopulation", *Ramparts* (Aug.-Sept. 1975), p. 59.

14. Alan S. Miller, "The Population Bomb Explodes at Home", *The Pacific Theological Review*, II,1 (Winter 1979), 4-12.

15. *Ibid.*, p. 6 citing Mahmood Mamdani, "The Myth of Population Control", *New York Monthly Review Press* (1973), p. 111.

16. Miller, "Population Bomb", p. 8 citing Alan Berg, "The Role of Nutrition in National Development", *Technology Review* (Feb. 1970), pp. 45-51.

17. Miller, "Population Bomb", p. 7 citing Narendra Singh, "Overpopulation is No Excuse", *Ceres* (May/June 1976), p. 59.

18. Thoreau celebrated his escape from society in *Walden or Life in the Woods* (Boston, 1854).

19. Picht, *Prognose*, p. 52.

20. Charles Birch, "Nature, Humanity and God in Ecological Perspective", *Faith and Science in an Unjust World,* 2 vols. (Geneva, 1980), I, 72 f. The volume contains the plenary presentations of the World Council of Churches' Conference on Faith, Science and the Future.

21. In *The Iron Sun,* Berry devotes a chapter to "the politicians who try to make political capital out of stopping a project to create a "black hole", a light-year distant from the earth. Only by subterfuge, by reporting the progress of the project only after it moves beyond control toward its own completion, are the scientists able to "escape" the politicians' ability to shut down the effort as they shut down the American SST. Berry's scientists, of course, save the race. The chapter bears consideration, however, because it is exactly such subterfuge that makes science and technology both suspect and extremely dangerous. The scientist thus becomes not only omnipotent but omniscient as well, and perhaps also omnidestructive. Berry, *Iron Sun,* pp. 103 ff.

22. Picht, *Bedingungen des Friedens,* p. 36.

23. Howe notes that the lecture was delivered in 1938; the text of the lecture itself, published in Max Planck, *Vorträge und Erinnerungen* (Darmstadt, 1975), dates the lecture May, 1937.

24. Planck, *Vorträge,* pp. 332 f.

25. *Ibid.,* pp. 319 f.

26. *Ibid.*

27. *Ibid.,* p. 330.

28. *Ibid.,* p. 333.

29. Howe, *Christenheit,* p. 335.

30. The Confessing Church *(Die Bekennende Kirche)* was the part of the Church which refused to submit to Hitler's dictates and continued to be critical of the Nazi policies right through and to the end of the war even at the cost of concentration camp and death.

31. Howe, *Christenheit,* p. 30. Howe uses excerpts from Karl Barth, *Kirchliche Dogmatik* I/1, 3-9. The English translation of Barth's passage is found in the *Church Dogmatics,* I/1 (Second Edition), pp. 4-6.

32. Howe, *Christenheit,* p. 30. Cf. above references to Brunner's attempt to propagate a "Natural Theology", pp. 131 ff. Thus Barth's theology was directly responsible not only for the revival of biblical theology and the theology of the Reformation; the impetus of his theology is responsible for the current ecumenical interest in the dialogue between theology and science as well.

33. *Ibid.,* p. 34.

34. Cf. *ibid.,* pp. 32 ff.

35. Letter dated October 14, 1948, *ibid.,* p. 343.

36. *Ibid.,* pp. 344 f.

37. *Ibid.,* p. 344.

38. Busch, *Karl Barth,* p. 340. Busch notes a letter of Barth's indicating that Gogarten was present at a lecture which Barth held in Göttingen in 1946, ". . . I thought it better that we shouldn't speak, because nothing could come of it", "Conversations with Wuppertal Students, 1 July 1968".

39. Howe, *Christenheit,* p. 345.

180   THEOLOGY AND SCIENCE IN MUTUAL MODIFICATION

40. Weizsäcker cited by Howe, *ibid.,* pp. 344 f.
41. *Ibid.,* p. 345.
42. *Ibid.*
43. This division made by Ockham, in spite of its fatal consequences today, was probably necessary at the time to break the Church's stranglehold on scientific thought.
44. World Council of Churches Council Report, "The Church in Europe and the Crisis of Modern Man" (Geneva, 1962).
45. The two volume conference report has appeared under the title *Faith and Science in an Unjust World,* eds. Robert L. Shinn and Paul Albrecht (Geneva, 1980).
46. Cf. a notice of the Karl-Heim-Gesellschaft in Karl Heim, *Die Wandlung im Naturwissenschaftlichen Weltbild* (Wuppertal, 1975), p. 260.
47. Cf. Ian S. Barbour, *Issues in Science and Religion* (Englewood Cliffs, 1966) and Harold Schilling, *The New Consciousness in Science and Religion* (London, 1973).
48. Notable also in this regard is the Templeton Foundation Prize for Progress in Religion which on two different occasions was given for work done in the field of religion and natural science. The Prize, which is sponsored by the Templeton Foundation, and which at present is the largest of its kind in the world, was awarded in 1978 to Professor Thomas F. Torrance and in 1980 to Professor Ralph Burhoe in recognition of their rather different contributions toward a new understanding between religion and science.
49. "The First Yearly Report of the Christophorus Stift, 1948", cited by Howe, *Christenheit,* p. 331.
50. Martin Heidegger, *Holzwege* (Frankfurt/M, 1950), pp. 69-89.
51. Cf. above pp. 36 ff., 142 ff.
52. Günter Howe, *Gespräch zwischen Theologie und Physik, Glaube und Forschung* (Gladbeck, 1950), II, 157.
53. Meschkowski, *Christentum,* p. 95.
54. P. B. Medawar, *The Hope of Progress* (London, 1972), p. 107.
55. The "closed universe" has given way to the "open universe".
56. Cf. the essays by C. F. von Weizsäcker, "Materie und Bewusstsein", *Die Einheit der Natur* (München, 1972), pp. 313-319, and "Materie, Energie, Information", *ibid.,* pp. 342-366.
57. T. F. Torrance, *Theology in Reconciliation* (London, 1975), p. 270.
58. Bonhoeffer, *Widerstand und Ergebung,* p. 182.
59. Howe, *Christenheit,* p. 84.
60. Howe, *Gott und die Technik,* p. 23.
61. Howe, *Christenheit,* p. 49.
62. Heidegger, *Holzwege,* p. 300.
63. Klaus Koch, "The Old Testament View of Nature", *Anticipation,* 25 (January, 1979), 49.
64. Lynn White, "The Historical Roots of Our Ecologic Crisis", *Science,* 155, No. 3767 (March, 1967), 1207.
65. Martin Heidegger cited by Howe, *Christenheit,* p. 197.
66. Nelson, *Science and Our Troubled Conscience,* pp. 72 ff.

67. Claus Westermann, *Genesis, Kapitel 1-11*, (Neukirchen, 1974), pp. 219 f. and Norbert Lohfink, *Unsere grossen Wörter* (Freiburg, 1977), pp. 167 ff., esp. p. 169.
68. Koch, "Old Testament View", p. 129.
69. Shinn and Albrecht, eds., *Faith and Science*, I, 31-40; II, 7-27.
70. *Ibid.*, II, 16.

Index of Persons

Index of Subjects